UNCHARTED

SUPRISING LESSONS FROM BUSINESS LEADERS.

RAAM ANAND et. al.

STARDOM BOOKS

www.StardomBooks.com

STARDOM BOOKS
112 Bordeaux Ct.
Coppell, TX 75019, USA

FIRST EDITION JUNE 2024

STARDOM BOOKS, LLC.
112 Bordeaux Ct. Coppell, TX 75019, USA
www.stardombooks.com

Stardom Books, United States
Stardom Alliance, India

The author and publishers have made all reasonable efforts to contact copyright holders for permission and apologize for any omissions or errors in the form of credits given. Corrections may be made to future editions.

UNCHARTED / Surprising Lessons from Business Leaders
Stardom Alliance

p. 157

cm. 13.5 X 21.5

Category:

BUS046000 - Business & Economics : Motivational

BUS025000 - Business & Economics : Entrepreneurship

SEL021000 - Self-Help : Motivational & Inspirational

ISBN: 978-1-957456-52-2

DEDICATION

This book is dedicated to all those amazing souls who had the guts and perseverance to overcome the insurmountable challenges that life threw at them and survived successfully to tell their stories of struggles, successes and triumphs, in this book. No wonder it's called "Uncharted!

DISCLAIMER

The views, opinions and information presented in this book are from the co-authors of the publication. The publisher does not endorse or subscribe to the information; reader discretion is solicited.

This book is designed to provide information on how each one of the co-authors did what they did, as their own personal narrative. It is sold with the understanding that neither the co-authors nor the publisher is engaged in rendering legal, accounting or other professional services. If legal or other professional advice is warranted, the services of an appropriate professional should be sought. Also, this book cannot be an exhaustive and complete presentation on the topics within the book. While every effort has been made to make the information presented here as complete and accurate as possible, it may contain errors, omissions or information that was accurate as of its publication but subsequently has become outdated by marketplace or industry changes or conditions, new laws or regulations, or other circumstances.

Neither the co-authors nor the publisher accepts any liability or responsibility to any person or entity with respect to any loss or damage alleged to have been caused, directly or indirectly, by the information, ideas, opinions or other content in this book. If you do not agree to these terms, you should immediately return this book for full refund.

NOTE FROM THE PUBLISHER

It was a great pleasure to work with all the CO-AUTHORS of this book to bring out their stories, perspectives and insights on how they did what they did.

Each one of them have gone through their own struggles, overcome challenges and successfully steered their businesses and careers into becoming a well-known names in their respective industries.

Through this publication, I wanted to bring out their views so that you, the reader can benefit and get inspired by their achievements. The experts were specifically asked to share how they did what they did and their message to the world.

So, here it is, for not just your reading pleasure, but also as a reference guide to help you shorten the learning curve and outshine in your own personal endeavors.

As you are going to learn by reading from the contributors of this book, you will understand that all of them have one common thing to say... TAKE ACTION.

Go ahead, read the book, take action and bring about a positive difference in your life, business and career – today!

RAAM ANAND, PUBLISHER.

CONTENTS

ACKNOWLEDGMENTS

You have seen them often. You pick up a book and get to this section, and find that the author, once again, has dedicated the book to someone else and not you. Some unknown, non-existent assistant or some casual reference to famous people.

Not this time.

I would like to thank YOU for taking time to get this book. I would be even more grateful if you read the book and take ACTION to further your life and create a positive difference.

1

CONQUERING THE UNKNOWN – THE INSPIRATIONAL TALE OF ENTREPRENEURIAL TRIUMPH

BY

DR. SANTOSH BATNI

"Success is not final, failure is not fatal: it is the courage to continue that counts."

– Winston Churchill

"Life is a journey. Not a destination."— This seemingly simple statement is rich in meaning, capturing the essence of life's endless adventures and experiences. It suggests that the value of life does not lie in arriving at a particular destination but rather in the moments and lessons learned throughout the journey. In this journey, there will be many pleasant and unsatisfactory chapters. But no matter what happens, it is vital never to stop turning the page because every chapter teaches something new. I believe we are travelers traveling through the endless adventures that life offers. However, every

individual has a different experience, destination, and itinerary to tick off. As I sit here today, attempting to distill my experiences of "The journey of an employee to an employer" into a unified narrative, I find myself confronted with the sheer enormity of my life's journey. Reflecting on it feels like peering into an infinitely complex kaleidoscope, each tiny reflective shard representing a different moment or lesson contributing to my life's rich tapestry.

In a world where economic disparities persist like deep chasms and opportunities appear as elusive as a mirage in the desert, countless individuals find themselves trapped within the suffocating confines of their circumstances. Amidst the depths of their struggles, a flicker of hope beckons—a chance to break free from the shackles of the past and harbor a future brimming with possibility. Like many other individuals, I— Dr. Santosh Batni- vowed to dedicate myself to a disciplined life full of hard work and achieve tremendous success no matter what hindrances come my way.

Hailing from a lower-middle-class family, I did not have the luxury of experiencing the fancy aspects of childhood. From studying in an underprivileged school to attaining a Diploma in Engineering from Oxford Polytechnic to graduating from Dayanand Sagar College in Civil Engineering, and further getting a PhD from California Public University— it was an enormous change in my life. Today, I firmly believe that your circumstances never define who you are. If you believe in yourself, work hard, and acquire the skills to thrive, you will emerge victorious. I say this with conviction because, as a child, I always aspired to be a Civil Engineer. As a student, the biggest lesson I learned was that there is no substitute for hard work or, as Beverly Sills rightly states, *"There are no shortcuts to anyplace worth going."*

In 2004, I was offered campus placement at an Engineering firm as a Trainee Engineer. With a twinkle in the eye and fire in my heart, I began the second phase of my journey as an employee. A lot of hard work occupied the next six years of my life, and my performance stood out from the crowd. However, I did not receive my fair share of recognition.

To be honest, this bothered me vehemently as I have always been a dedicated and hardworking person, and not being credited for my ideas and performance seemed underwhelming. Since then, I wanted to do something on my own. Several minor improvements could have been made concerning our scope of work, but I needed to be empowered to suggest or make those changes within the organization.

Nevertheless, I continued to put endless efforts into my role and excelled. I diligently met project deadlines with utmost sincerity and continued to upskill myself with every passing day. As we know, life is never a bed full of roses. There will be several obstacles on the way, and I had my fair share of battles to fight, too. In 2010 the international market started collapsing due to the global economic crisis and the organization where I was employed did not have a project for a long time and as time passed by like a flowing river we had to shut down with a heavy heart.

All of a sudden, one fine day, I got a call from one of my Canadian customers who was working with me. He informed me that they needed somebody to take care of their projects. He trusted us as I worked as a Project Manager and directly answered client calls. I found a ray of hope amidst all the maddening chaos. To me, this was a great opportunity wherein I could build upon the six years of knowledge and competence that I had gained. Albeit a little anxious about the unknown, I was equally excited about giving this a shot. I wanted to walk the path less traveled. In fact, I have come across a quote that said, "It's hard to fail but it is worse never to have tried to succeed." These words have since become a mural on the walls of my mind.

Much like a river carving its own path through the land, my life's journey has meandered away from the well-trodden road, instead seeking the thrill of the unexplored, continually asking, "How can I do this differently?" This mental compass has steered me towards the land of innovation and self-improvement. Therefore, after an elaborate discussion with my wife (who was also my colleague in my first organization), I felt it would be better to go a step ahead, use my skill sets, and build an organization of my own in my area of expertise. I was exhilarated as I finally could be an entrepreneur. I could finally call something my own, which I built from scratch with my sweat and blood— That is how **"Brainstorm Infotech"** was born, with a team of five engineers. The universe paved the situation in such a way that I was pushed in the right direction, and it proved to be a blessing for me. Initially, I was a little unsure of how this change would work and the consequences since it required an initial investment in infrastructure and skilled people.

As mentioned, we embarked upon this new chapter of our lives with five engineers, who were my trusted ex-colleagues. The North American market situation started improving in 2011-2012. More clients began to approach us to collaborate on new projects. The business started excelling even in the US and in Canada. People started investing in construction, and my previous clients started approaching me. I started picking up some projects, but that was when we had a financial crunch because we did not have enough resources to invest. It required costly software, so we started working double shifts with the same team and made a little money to invest more in the infrastructure. As time progressed, we thought of expanding our workforce even more because working 16-18 hours daily was challenging.

Since we wanted this business to thrive, we wanted to invest more, leading us to move to a commercial space with a capacity of around 20 to 25 seaters. We started hiring freshers from college and began training them. To state it humbly, my team and I took the responsibility of technical training. In this way, we hired around 50 employees. The new team members were trained with Canadian and American standards. With time, our team grew significantly, and we had about 200 accommodations. Today, after a decade, we can accommodate 400 people and have around 200 engineers working with us. Our belief in continuous learning and improvement made us execute projects with finesse and accuracy. As a team, we believe in our pillars of success— **Teamwork, Integrity, Commitment,**

Courage, and Perseverance. This led me to commit to this beautiful journey fully.

I always believed in steady growth, rather than investing a lot early and losing money, which has led to a consistent growth of 20-30% year on year since 2011. There were a few challenges, too, but we never gave up. No matter how much you try, there will always be hurdles. It is up to you whether you want to use them as a burning desire for motivation or as excuses for failure. During that time, my financial liabilities and commitments were small. Therefore, it was easy to maintain employee salaries and infrastructure. However, after growing ten times ahead of where we used to be, the expenses have started growing, too. Now, we are ahead of the survival process. To be rational, people work at offices to get salaries. Therefore, they will leave as soon as you stop paying them because everyone has to feed their families. This is one of the biggest concerns when you start as an entrepreneur.

You are bummed with thoughts like— "How do I arrange the next month's salary?" Today, with some clients who have worked with us for around a decade, we know how much revenue we get from them on average every year. So, when you start growing— at some stage, you will begin to expand beyond the survival stage and then delve into the development or growth stage. Since this is a very competitive market, it is vital to know where you stand. When I started my career, this industry was small, with few detailing companies in India.

Today, there are a lot of small companies in India that have been acquired by large engineering companies in the US. Therefore, when foreign money comes into the infrastructure and development, it becomes a game-changer. It is not easy to compete with them. However, with our experience, competence, and quality of work, our growth in the last 14 years has been steady, and we have been getting ample projects.

It is very natural for unknown people to not confide in you. Similarly, clients, too, need some reassurance to lay their trust in you. If there is an error, they lose big time because the fabricators directly fabricate steel based on our design and detailing, and the erectors blindly start erecting from our drawings. It is not the drawing that goes; it is actual steel. It is essential to maintain accuracy in our drawings. However, if there is any error while erecting the structure, it results in significant back charges, which include the cost of— refabrication, transportation to the site, and erection delays since the fabrication shop is miles away from the construction site. Therefore, everything needs to be pre-engineered accurately. When you start to get repeat business, you learn better about your client's choices and what is convenient for them. This way, we became fabricator-friendly and never lost a client in the last fourteen years. Furthermore, this year, we are having our company exhibition booth at the NASCC(2024) in San Antonio, Texas, USA, which allows us to meet all our potential customers.

As we know, life is a journey marked by unpredictability, akin to navigating through an ocean in the darkness of the night, where challenges loom ominously like turbulent storm clouds, ready to unleash their torrent upon the unsuspecting traveler at any given moment. Although these trials and tribulations might bruise our spirits and test the limits of our resilience, they are fundamental elements of our existence, as integral as the stars scattered across the celestial canopy. Attempting to evade these challenges is as futile as trying to outrun your shadow; the further you sprint, the longer it stretches, persistently trailing your every move, a spectral echo of your form. Like any other entrepreneur, I faced ups and downs in the business, too, but the dawn of COVID-19 was the most challenging phase. It was a nightmare. One fine day, out of the blue, everyone received a notice from the government that there would be a complete lockdown the next day. With COVID-19 cases and death rates increasing every day, our lives and business had become highly challenging, and compared to working from an office location, working from a satellite office presented a new challenge for the entire team. We had to make a decision and refrain from working from the office.

At that time, I had a 75-member team, and around 60 teammates returned to their hometowns the same night. Most people needed access to a laptop or desktop to work with, even if they wanted to work from their hometown. I was clueless and did not know how to handle this situation. The North American market was functional since the construction industry came under essential services, which meant that existing projects were to be completed on time and new projects kept coming in, which took a lot of work to manage. We needed to prepare to facilitate work from home. We were under tremendous pressure, and with all the obstacles that we were facing, we reached a point where we needed help to sustain our operations. There was also a huge financial implication for any delay in the completion of projects. The Construction industry was operational, though it was slow. Project delays usually come with substantial back charges since we agree with the client to complete their projects within agreed deadlines. Thankfully, our clients understood the situation and were flexible to allow us more time. This encouraged us to go the extra mile.

Working from home became more challenging for me than COVID-19, so my team and I went to each remote employee's location and delivered all the infrastructure like computer systems, worktables, and the internet that helped them work from home. My Project Managers and I would be on calls for nearly twenty hours a day, talking to all team members working on various projects to ensure all the projects were executed accurately and on time.

The support of my employees gave me a tremendous amount of confidence. Even though it was a slow process, we tried to manage this complex situation. Within a few months, around 60% of my staff returned to work. To ensure hygiene and safety, we always wore masks and even provided accommodation to people who needed them.

We were forced to make bold decisions unconventionally as COVID-19 gripped and caused turmoil in the world. This really helped us to work around the new normal. With some of our employees reporting back to work slowly, our productivity, communication, and efficiency improved significantly in executing projects as per customer delivery standards. When the second wave of COVID-19 hit, we were better prepared to deal with the challenge since we had made all the required changes to facilitate work continuity, whether in office space or from home. It was all about adapting to the situation. After all, not everything happens the way you plan. Going with the flow and trusting your gut helps a lot of times. But no matter what, those two years of lockdown were quite devastating. Our business neither grew much nor did it fail during these two years. We were in a straight line— neither did we have any profit nor any loss. But somehow, we managed, and both our employees and customers appreciated our commitment. Everything eventually worked out. The lessons that COVID-19 taught us were valuable. Giving up and losing faith in the face of adversity is an alien concept to me and my team. This experience taught us to take measures to deal with similar crises in the future.

Despite achieving significant milestones, I could re-integrate or return to the "ordinary world" due to the post-COVID scenario. The new normal brought several changes in our lives. We looked more at finding solutions to each challenge rather than being consumed by it. I also believe there is nothing called the "Biggest goal," as success is a journey and a moving goalpost. We are happy about our achievements, but there is still a long way to go. In all the successes that we have achieved so far, it is essential to practice **"Professional Will and Personal Humility."** For all the words that the universe can bestow me with, **Gratitude** is the word I will always have for every opportunity I have been blessed with. The team with whom I laid the foundation of my organization are senior project managers now. Today, they handle multiple projects of various complexities, sizes, and scales across North America and the Middle East.

I currently invest my time in marketing, managing, and upskilling the organization. My next goal is to keep growing exponentially and steadily. Even though no organization can make everyone happy, I always tell my Project Managers that employees are our top priority and should feel connected to the organization. Employees should feel respected and work passionately, not just for the money. We started with this vision and still follow the same culture. This is why our employees supported us through all the hardships, especially during COVID-19, because they had the same vision and dream. Today, each one has grown professionally and personally, and I couldn't have been happier. They trusted me when this journey began. To me, the most significant achievement in life is— Gaining the trust of all my employees and making their leap of faith worthwhile.

Apart from these professional challenges, specific personal challenges also occurred in the course of time. I overlooked my physical health since I was so invested in the company. I started facing a few health issues. I did not focus on balancing my personal and professional life. At this age, taking care of your mental and physical health is essential because, after a specific time, you will not have the energy to work on yourself from scratch. With this epiphany, I understood how I was unknowingly pressurizing my mind and body; I decided to bring in a change. Therefore, I started focusing on my physical and mental health— meditating, going to the gym, and dedicating an hour of badminton practice became an essential daily routine. Earlier, I worked every day, but now I relax on weekends, listen to music, and spend time with my family and friends. In the same way, I now encourage my employees to have a balance between their personal and professional lives.

In the last fourteen years, we have gained much experience overcoming multitudes of challenges. Both success and challenges have taught us belief, resilience, patience, courage to change, humility, and perseverance. The goal will always be to implement all the wisdom I have gained in all these years. People are your most incredible resource and strength; when ordinary people work as a team, one can achieve extraordinary results. When I started this journey, I was more a part of it as much as my team was. After over fourteen years, now that I have a clear vision and direction, I lead this journey with gratitude to build a better future. What started with a tiny group of five engineers has grown into a significantly large team. Over the last fourteen years of immense hard work and multi-tasking, we have executed over 2750 projects in North America and the Middle East. I aim to give my best efforts every day and help as many people as I can. This journey has made me wiser and taught me to accept every challenge as an opportunity towards something new— This applies to both personal and professional life.

"Brainstorm Infotech" has been recognized and featured as:

- One of the "Top 10 Structural Steel Design and Detailing Companies in 2020" By Industry Outlook Business magazine.
- The "Leading Emerging Indian Company of the Year Award" From the Indian Economic Development & Research Association in April 2021.
- One of the "10 Most Prominent Structural Steel Design and Detailing Companies in 2021" by Silicon India Business Magazine.
- The "Fastest Growing Indian Company Excellence Award" at the International Achievers Conference in 2021.
- "Leaders in Structural Steel Design" in 2021 By CEO Insights Business Magazine.
- In 2021, we got another International Achievers Award as "The Fastest Growing Indian Company" by National Economic Development & Social Responsibilities.
- "Top 10 Leaders in Structural Design" By CEO Insights. In the year 2022, we once again got awarded "Outstanding Business Leadership" for excellence in Structural Steel Design by the International Business Conclave in Thailand in 2022.
- "The Most Promising Steel Detailing Company" by Business Connect & Indo-Global Entrepreneurship Forum in 2024.
- "The Mahatma Gandhi Samman" (NRI Welfare Society of India) at the House of Commons, London, UK, in 2022.
- I was also awarded a fellowship by the Indian Institute of Engineers in 2023.

We are profoundly grateful and humbled to receive multiple awards over the passage of time. Being recognized for our quality of work after building everything from scratch gives us immense joy and happiness. If I could offer advice to a budding entrepreneur or someone about to embark on a similar journey, there is no substitute for hard work. You have to put in the hours that are needed. There is no shortcut to success. You must be diligent, extremely dedicated, and ready to face all kinds of situations. Whatever I do, I always do it passionately. Therefore, I always suggest doing what you are passionate about very sincerely. You have to build, trust, and develop your team. Patience and perseverance are the keys to success— It does not come overnight. There will be ups and downs, but obstacles cannot stop you from achieving what you want. Apart from professional goals, it would help to dedicate yourself to your physical and mental health. Do not dwell on your mistakes, and always look for a better tomorrow. Believe in your vision, inspire the people around you, and, most importantly, practice gratitude.

As we navigate the convoluted labyrinth of life, gaining profound clarity about one's desires and embodying an unabashed self-awareness is vital. The tower of genuine relationships can only be achieved on the bedrock of honesty; the deceptive illusion of pretense causes it to crumble like a sandcastle against an unforgiving tide. Therefore, you must be clear about what you want and always have honest intentions. You can have all the achievements in your life, but at the end of the day, the only thing that matters is— how you made the people around you feel and how you treated them. You can pay your employees tons of salaries, but if you don't treat them well, misbehave with them, and make them feel less of a human being, they will never respect you or even be dedicated to your vision. Therefore, ask yourself— "How can I be good? How can I continue to be good within all challenges and still ensure I do the right thing and treat my people with dignity?" This is the core requirement to be remembered as a good human being and leave a legacy.

A huge part of my success is attributed to the support given by my better half, Vidhya Santosh, who is also a civil engineer and currently a part of the admin team. She was my backbone emotionally and pushed me at every stage to pursue this dream, even though it demanded a lot of personal sacrifices. I owe my success to her as well. Furthermore, the credit also goes to my entire team that continues to believe and trust in me and our vision. They shared and continue to give the same level of commitment to our vision to live, lead, and leave a legacy, which confirmed my confidence in this challenging journey. When this journey started, the focus was to sustain, build upon it, and evolve based on experiences and learnings. My mentors and support systems have given me the best advice I follow even today— a) Keep in mind to create a "win-win" situation for yourself and the customer. b) Be prepared to manage and overcome pressure situations during project execution. c) Lastly, learn from your mistakes, not repeat them.

Today, as I reflect upon my journey, I cannot help but feel a sense of pride for the twenty-year-old employee in me who stood tall amidst the turbulent winds of challenges and uncertainty to reach where he is today. My experience of "the journey of an employee to an employer" is not a whimsical tale of instant success or a formulaic blueprint promising a life devoid of challenges. Instead, it is a testament to the indomitable human spirit—the resilience, determination, and unwavering belief that can shape destinies. If my journey can offer a roadmap to navigate the labyrinth of life, empowering even one person to seize opportunities, conquer obstacles, and script their own extraordinary stories. In that case, it will make me the happiest. Whether you are an aspiring entrepreneur, a professional seeking to unleash your full potential or an individual yearning for change, I pray you believe in your dreams and paint your canvas the way you want. All said and done, though I firmly believe that **"The Experience cannot be Explained,"** I have tried my best to capture the same in words. You would have heard a popular saying, **"THE JOURNEY HAS JUST BEGUN."**

AUTHOR BIO

With over 20 years of experience in the industry, Dr. Santosh Batni is an expert in providing end-to-end solutions in steel design and detailing services. Founded Brainstorm Infotech in 2010 and spearheaded its tremendous growth in the last decade, thereby being recognized as one of the top 10 steel detailing companies in India.

He has been awarded an Honorary Doctorate in Engineering from the California Public University in June 2021. Dr. Santosh Batni is also a fellow of the Institution of Engineers, India since 2023.

Dr. SANTOSH BATNI, CO-AUTHOR

2

THE UNSTOPPABLE SERIAL ENTREPRENEUR

BY

NARENDRA RAM

"Arise, awake and stop not till the goal is reached."

– Swami Vivekananda

People usually believe that if you are good at something, you should always try to stick to it and make a living from its mastery, using the saying, "Jack of all trades, master of none," to shame others into following a weather-beaten path. All our lives, we are told to achieve excellence in one field and be known for that. Everyone craves stability and the comfort of complacency, but I was never such a person. On the contrary, I was infamous for frequently shifting gears and jumping from one phase of life to another. Variety is the spice of life, they say, and I do not disagree at all! Why do only one thing when you can do many things at once? So, I broke the norm and tried my hands at many roles until I found myself drawn to a field where I had never imagined I would build a business empire.

This is my story: the story of a multipotentialite boy who walked on many different roads in his life, only to end up heeding his true calling as a pioneering entrepreneur. As I continue to fulfill my destiny and dream big, I wish to inspire you with my journey. I want you to know that if I could make a difference in this bustling world, so can you.

Here's how I did it, dear reader!

The Beginning of it All

The first chapter of my life started in the bustling state of Andhra Pradesh, where I was born to doting parents who always ensured I was loved and cared for. My mother was gentle, but, in stark contrast, my father was a strict disciplinarian. I still wonder how I managed to escape his wrath as a naughty kid! Thanks to them, I had a happy childhood, making the most of what I had and not cribbing about what I didn't.

Although it seems unlikely, I was indeed a full-fledged backbencher, and I am not the least bit ashamed of admitting that. I could never quietly sit through a class like a robot or soak up everything the teachers taught like a sponge. So, I would be physically present in my designated seat, but my heart and mind would be frolicking on the sports ground of my school. Every day, I would wake up exactly at 4 am even without an alarm bell and be off to the morning practice sessions. After the school hours whizzed past, I would attend the evening practice with full enthusiasm, often reaching home late and falling straight into bed. Luckily, despite my hectic schedule, I'd always pass all my exams, attending various tournaments and competitions whenever I could. Besides, my exceptional athletic abilities made up for whatever I lacked in academics.

That is how I became a district champion in table tennis, an ace sprinter in the 100 m, 200 m, and 400 m categories, and the most reliable player for the school-level volleyball and football teams, all within a few years. My most prized achievement in sports, though, is becoming the captain of the Under-13 district cricket team of that time, later getting selected to play for the state cricket team, and then representing the entire south zone as the Vice Captain. The thrill of leading the teams I captained to victory and seeing my efforts bear fruit is still alive and well in my memories. Naturally, I had an immensely fulfilling life when I was in school, and the shelves of my home still proudly hold all the medals and trophies I won back then.

As life would have it, in the blink of an eye, it was time for me to leave my carefree years behind and transition into adulthood. I was initially apprehensive about college life because I hadn't put much effort into my studies, and I wondered if I could secure admission anywhere. That is where my exceptional achievements in sports came to my rescue, and I was granted a second chance to take my education seriously. With perseverance and persistence, I obtained a Bachelor's Degree in Commerce and secured admission to the MBA program of the reputed Institute of Public Enterprise, which is still one of the best management institutes in Hyderabad. But I did not want to stop there. So, I pursued a Bachelor's Degree in Law and a Post-graduate Diploma in Communication and Journalism. After completing my studies, I decided to cease my academic pursuits and mentally prepare myself for the professional world, like most of my peers. In hindsight, I think the seeds of my entrepreneurial journey were sown while pursuing my MBA, and whatever I learned then came to great use later in life.

A Box Full of Surprises

Let me ask you a question, dear reader. Why do you think someone goes to college and pursues higher education? Your answer might be anything from "for the love of knowledge" to "just for fun," but back then, there was only one reason: to land the best-paying and most secure job possible. Having completed my MBA in 2001, I knew that fresh graduates like me were being offered career opportunities in the IT sector due to the IT surge of the new millennium. Naturally, college placements and preparatory classes were highly sought after.

Everyone was running the rat race and accepting any remotely lucrative offer that came their way; my classmates and peers did, too. Most of them managed to be placed in established organizations and MNCs. But fate had wildly different plans for me because I wasn't placed in any organization whatsoever. Due to some inexplicable reason, I was one of those very few students who weren't crazy about having to get a job. I put as much effort into all the placement activities as I saw fit, leaving the rest up to chance. But it was a bolt out of the blue when I didn't secure even one placement, even as a fluke. A possible gap year stared me in the face, and I remained unemployed for eight months after graduation.

Although I had every chance of wasting all that time, I started to concoct various business plans and ideas with the full intention of starting my venture. My parents, unfortunately, caught wind of my plans and tried to talk me out of it; they weren't entirely keen on me completely forsaking the corporate world. I remember them coaxing me to get a job and work for a few years, then softening the blow by saying I could start a business later if I wanted to. I eventually gave in and began to search for jobs.

After a tough time encountering job opportunities that I didn't particularly like, I joined a respected HR outsourcing and consulting firm as an HR trainee. Now, this organization that I joined as an HR trainee was a leading name in the field of IP networking and had multiple branches all across the country. I was pretty pumped about taking charge of a great deal of responsibilities as part of a team, but there was a catch: my boss had told me that I would not receive a salary for six months and that I'd be paid only after that period. I still believe anyone else in my place would have stepped back, but I accepted the offer, determined to take this challenge head-on and commit myself to my work. So, although I felt apprehensive, I did my best without letting the uncertainty get to me. Much to my relief, I was promptly handed a sum of three thousand rupees as my first salary at the end of the six months, and that was officially my first-ever salary.

Three thousand rupees might not amount to much today, but it meant the whole world to me back then. I remember that the first things I bought with that money were a saree for my dear mother and a blue watch for myself. It was the most surreal feeling to realize that I was earning and could afford to give myself small rewards from time to time, and my determination to become financially independent was strengthened five-fold. I never looked back after that. I kept putting my best foot forward at work. Within the span of a few years, I received massive hikes in my salary, performance incentives, and a slew of promotions that ultimately made me the HR manager of the whole organization. When I finally left my job towards the end of 2006, I had the respect of scores of colleagues and superiors, some of whom became my close associates later.

One thing was clear to me during this brief foray into the corporate world. Professional competence and inner peace are crucial for becoming a better person, attaining greater heights in life, and thriving in a world of cutthroat competition. The lessons I learned from three people helped me acquire all the essential values in my life; I still look up to them. The first person is Mr. GR Reddy, founder and MD of Husys Consulting Limited. Everything I know about financial management and public relations, I learned from him; in fact, he also taught me the importance of patience in business. He was always quite adept at handling everything related to finances effortlessly, and his deep appreciation for human connection and communication imprinted itself on me. The second figure I count as an ally is Mr. P Sridhar Reddy, founder, and CEO of CtrlS and Cloud4C. Whenever we've had a conversation, he has motivated me primarily with his passion for work and life. His professional journey inspires me, and he is someone from whom I have learned practical team management skills. The third person from whom I learned the most significant life lessons—how to be connected with the Almighty, to be humble and grounded, to be calm and patient through the ups and downs of life, and the importance of meditation—is Mr. K Siva Prasad. He is a serving bureaucrat and one of the most competent professionals I have ever met.

Armed with everything I learned from these three figures, I decided to inaugurate a new chapter in my life: finally answering my destiny's call and doing what I was always meant to do.

Inching Towards the Dream

In 2006, driven by my inner fire, I confidently charted a trajectory for myself to kickstart my entrepreneurship journey. I first started a company called IT Curve, a professional IT training firm that equips young executives and office workers with training in IT skills, soft skills, and other essential professional skills. Then, I invested in other education-centered companies called Asian Pacific and Edumind, which conducted educational programs at the university level by tying up with several renowned universities and institutes across India. I was also instrumental in developing and streamlining the franchisee model for the entire company. In those days alone, the company had over 1500 franchises and over one lakh students enrolled in various courses. Soon enough, as a measure to adapt to changing times, Asian Pacific also introduced hardware- and software-oriented programs, which were very successful.

Along the way, I also forayed into the media sector in 2010 when I became the Managing Partner of Power Politics, one of India's most famous political magazines. I was grateful to have had many stalwarts in media and journalism work with the company on the magazine's editorial team. In the same year, I also started an infrastructure business through which I developed several properties of 2-3 lakh square feet each within just five years.

Always craving for more things to do and more places to be, 2012 saw me jumping back into the education sector with 195 Overseas Pvt. Ltd., a Hyderabad-based education consultancy. This consultancy helps aspirants upgrade their careers with lucrative degrees from over one hundred reputed universities in the USA, the UK, Australia, Canada, New Zealand, Ireland, Switzerland, and Singapore. 195 Overseas was my most ambitious project since I targeted foreign countries for students' higher education, and many risks were involved. Still, thankfully, business took off just fine, and we opened multiple branches in other states, too. This way, I established and became part of various businesses in under a decade, thriving under pressure and thoroughly enjoying every moment. It appeared that I had finally achieved my dream of becoming a successful first-generation entrepreneur. But this journey was far from over. I exited from this business in 2019 to concentrate on my new ventures.

I also worked as a consultant and on the boards of some of the biggest healthcare companies as an executive director to help them streamline their business operations. This helped me gain a deep insight into the opportunities available and the challenges the healthcare sector faced at that time. Later, while establishing Lifespan Private Limited, this experience helped me carve a successful venture.

Not so long after, while running all these ventures simultaneously and savoring prosperity at its best, I had an epiphany that would later lay the foundation for my true calling. 2014 was the year when, on one fine afternoon, on a very unremarkable day, it suddenly hit me— all the businesses I was running were creating good profit, but what about the people who were not benefiting from my work? What was I doing for the common folk, for the very same section of society in which I had my roots? That is when I changed course and established an NGO called FEEL Foundation, turning my wish into a solid action plan. Through the NGO, we've conducted all sorts of betterment programs: imparting education to the socially and economically marginalized, conducting more than 10,000 blood donation camps all over India, assisting multiple state governments in dealing with natural disasters such as draughts and floods, organizing women empowerment drives, and even inspiring thousands of people to pledge their eyes for donation.

Now, you might think that after accomplishing one milestone after the other, year after year, I must have had my fill of achievements and got my hands full with all the companies I was running. But the bug of inspiration bit me again. Then, I decided to do something entirely out of my comfort zone that would let me combine my passion for business with my mission of giving back to society, something I had never thought I would do until that one precious moment that changed the course of my life: I was going to set up my own nutraceuticals company!

The Wonder Called Lifespan

Still in pursuit of my dreams, I left my job in 2006 at the age of 26. Then, I decided to leave my home behind and shifted base to Delhi in the same year for a completely fresh start. It was a whole different ball game, adapting to a completely unfamiliar environment, language, and culture. Still, I took everything one step at a time and eventually acclimatized myself to the new life I was building. While in Delhi, I had my Eureka moment of starting a firm that would create nutritional supplements, now more popularly known as nutraceuticals, to aid people in living healthier and longer lives. What was that Eureka moment, you ask? Well, it arose from quite a simple story.

There is hardly anyone in India who isn't aware of Delhi's maddening pollution levels, which can make even the fittest of people terribly sick. Because of the same pollution, a busy and fast-paced lifestyle, and barely any time to look after myself, I started to fall ill quite often with one ailment or the other. It didn't help that I wasn't even eating properly. These circumstances also made me wonder how many Indians were undergoing the same suffering day in and day out, unknowingly shortening their lifespan with each passing day. I began to empathize with all these people, who, although not immediately visible, were very real and in the same boat as me, needing holistic nutritional care for their well-being.

It wasn't too long until things got worse and finally knocked some sense into my head: health is indeed the most accurate form of wealth, and I needed to ensure that this wealth would reach as many people as possible! So, one fine afternoon, on an otherwise uneventful day, I hatched the plan of starting my own nutraceutical company, and very cheekily, I christened it 'Lifespan'! I incubated this idea for years together, slowly learning about the art and science of starting and expanding businesses through my ventures. I committed every piece of relevant and vital information to my memory, learning skills such as resource management, better communication, and more along the way. But this alone wouldn't suffice.

I was used to handling media, education, and infrastructure ventures, but health and wellness? I was a frog that was merely beginning to step out of a well; I couldn't take a leap of faith just like that! I would need to know what I was getting myself into and do my homework, so, in my 30s, I threw myself into books, research papers, and everything else I could lay my hands on. I made some time out of my mind-numbingly busy schedule every day to study the texts of the Ayurveda and take pages after pages of notes. I educated myself about every leaf, bark, root, flower, and fruit that was instrumental in creating the most essential Ayurvedic formulations. I even pestered a few experts along the way, discussing what practices must always be adhered to.

Although I had gained plenty of know-how in nutraceuticals and Ayurveda, I had always firmly believed in the power of Mother Nature and the adage, "Let food be thy medicine." A simple explanatory analogy is this—no matter how many bandages you put on a burn wound, if the factor that caused that burn is still around, the wound won't heal. I also knew that nutraceutical supplements shouldn't be used as a replacement for a nourishing diet but rather as an addition to an already healthy lifestyle. Keeping all of this in mind, I slowly began to mentally prepare myself to let go of my inhibitions and leave the outcome of my endeavor to my potential customers.

Lifespan Private Limited, my most treasured brainchild, was born in 2016. Today, Lifespan is considered the most advanced and state-of-the-art facility in the country, which is way ahead of its time. The very first range of products created was related to sports nutrition, as I was very passionate about sports. I strongly wanted other sportspersons to have all the essential nutritional support they need to achieve peak performance naturally. So, we at Lifespan developed products such as whey protein, pre-workout drinks, and healthy snacks to provide the best nutritional support to sportspersons. After the initial line of products took off in both Telangana and Andhra Pradesh, I decided to initiate the second phase of action and launch a broader range of nutraceutical capsules, personal care products, health juices, health syrups, nutrition powders, effervescent tablets, and so on. For this, in 2017, the government of Telangana granted an area of 1,30,000 square feet to Lifespan in a prime location within Hyderabad to establish India's first and most extensive facility dedicated to nutraceutical manufacturing.

A few years later, Lifespan acquired an additional 500 acres of land dedicated to organic farming and to supply its Research and Development division with homegrown ingredients to develop new products. In 2018, Lifespan began to veer away from the known and established types of nutritional supplements and shift towards novel and pioneering formulations of its own, which later won the company multiple awards. 2019 saw the beginning of large-scale, full-fledged, independent production that turned the ambitious formulations into the final products that would reach consumers.

Today, Lifespan is among the leading producers of nutraceuticals and herbal, ayurvedic, and organic products in the health and wellness sectors. It is USFDA compliant and meets other standards such as the UKMHRA, TGA Australia, ISO, NSF, CGMP, Ayush, Ayush NABL certified, and many others. Today, Lifespan is one of India's largest, state-of-the-art, and most hygienic nutraceutical manufacturing facilities. Lifespan's products remain in great demand on e-commerce platforms such as Amazon and Flipkart and even in physical stores; they are so popular that when someone mentions 'nutrition' in the whole of Hyderabad, the first word that pops up is Lifespan.

We developed a pathbreaking product line in nutrition-based biscuits or edible disc-shaped nutritional snacks. We became the first nutraceutical company in the world to create biscuits made of the most iconic Ayurvedic immunity enhancer, Chyawanprash, apart from variants containing calcium, whey protein, etc. All of Lifespan's offerings are produced in manufacturing units that develop and market over 400 kinds of formulations, powered by a team of veteran scientists, expert technicians, and the best quality assurance professionals who form the organization's backbone. When you combine this power trio with top-notch facilities and the best pieces of equipment, the result is a brand that has begun to take not only India but also the world by storm!

At one glance, my interest in sports and educational background may appear starkly different from the career I chose to dedicate my life to. Although I did not stick to any of the career streams that people commonly pursue after the completion of any of these degrees, I realize today that everything I learned while I was studying these courses and even the little time I spent in the corporate sector came perfectly to my aid when I was setting up my business! So, even though life didn't show me the road straight ahead, it slowly guided me onto the road I was destined for. It makes me proud to say that I am one of India's youngest and most successful entrepreneurs and have received many accolades for my endeavors.

In 2019, Lifespan Pvt. Ltd. was awarded the Most Promising Company to Invest In (Health and Wellness sector) and Best Startup of the Year at the Global Indian Business Excellence Awards at the House of Commons in London. Apart from this, I was bestowed Young Entrepreneur of the Year in 2016 by the Times Group. In the same year, I was also presented with the Bharat Nirman Award for Economic Growth and Social Development by the Global Achiever Foundation, New Delhi, which recognizes and rewards social contributions by Indian entrepreneurs. I've also received multiple awards from various NGOs for being an active Society Representative. The brightest feather in my cap will always be seeing my face on the cover pages of various reputed financial and business magazines such as Forbes India, Outlook Business, Fortune India, Entrepreneur Magazine, Kama Insight, and many more. I, indeed, have come a long way from reading magazines to being featured in them.

Another feather of achievement in my success story was when the television channel History TV, one of the global leaders in TV media, created and broadcast an entire documentary on my life. They dedicated a full episode of 30 minutes to my journey, experiences, and achievements. People started looking up to me as their role model; I became a household name overnight. This newfound fame reminded me that I must fulfill my responsibilities and duties towards my people with never-ending sincerity and gusto.

Despite every other obstacle in my way, big or small, I've always managed to protect myself and my aspirations from falling apart. I have secured the future of all my ventures with my blood, sweat, and tears, so I believe I deserve all the success coming my way, savoring the joys while not letting them get to my head. Thanks to the fantastic present we at Lifespan are experiencing, I have already made plans stretching far into the future of the organization.

Regarding Lifespan's product line, we plan to launch low-calorie protein bars, nutritional gummies, and more varieties of nutrient biscuits. We have partnered with many general and modern Trade Retail store chains, and wish to expand to more retail stores. Soon enough, we will start franchises or branches of Lifespan in the UAE, the USA, and Europe; we will also introduce sub-brands like NLife, HealthySpan, Love Life, Agrispan, and more on five continents. Affected by the suffering inflicted upon humankind during the COVID-19 pandemic, my vision for the next five years is to develop Lifespan Hospitals in the entire country and open a chain of 1000+ Lifespan Pharmacies. We have already begun to work towards this goal and recently started with two hospitals in Hyderabad and ten pharmacy stores across Telangana and Andhra Pradesh. The blueprint of scaling up this vision across the country for both projects is almost ready to be implemented, too.

There are many more dreams I wish to fulfill, some jotted on paper and some etched in my mind, but one thing is sure: I will only stop once all my goals are achieved and shine on the list of my achievements.

The Hurdles I Overcame

No success story is ever complete or believable without a few significant obstacles thrown in. I, too, had to overcome my share of hurdles in order to achieve whatever I have achieved today. For starters, building the manufacturing unit for Lifespan's operations was like setting sail on wretched, unexplored seas. Owing to the lack of a sufficiently large crew or support staff, I collaborated directly with the small construction team involved with building the facilities for Lifespan and actively participated in every phase. I still remember how the pandemic struck our nation right as we had wrapped up construction; had we been just a month late, we would have suffered huge losses. All I had was the will and perseverance to help me stay afloat. But not having anyone to lean on for encouragement, let alone ground support, was a challenge that moved me deeply.

Throughout the time it took for me to bring Lifespan from paper to reality, I faced a lack of moral support from both family and friends. Everyone I discussed about setting up a pioneering nutraceuticals manufacturing unit in India dismissed me even before they heard my plans and vision. My family, friends, and well-wishers discouraged me from even laying the foundation for Lifespan. Their skepticism cast shadows of doubt over my aspirations, but I refused to let their uncertainty dim my resolve. Despite being a one-person army, I cast aside all my fears and decided to march alone, knowing that when the time was right, my family and friends would surely be proud of me.

Each encounter tested my patience and resolve as I navigated through the bureaucratic maze of government offices. I still remember vividly how, when I was applying for land to build Lifespan's headquarters and facilities, no one in the relevant government departments had ever heard the term 'nutraceutical.' So, my proposal sounded like gibberish to them, and they almost rejected it. I couldn't even imagine my plans ending up in a trashcan.

Out of desperation, I patiently explained the concept to them with as many relatable examples as possible. That is when they finally grasped my vision and allocated the required land to me. I persevered through it all, overcoming bureaucratic hurdles one piece of paperwork at a time.

Financial challenges loomed large, too, and these challenges had the most potential to throw my dreams completely off-track. Securing funds and convincing banks to extend loans for my mega-project initially seemed like scaling a mountain without any ropes. As an experienced entrepreneur, I knew I couldn't ask any of my peers for financial aid and would have to gather the resources required all by myself. So, with creative financing strategies and a steadfast belief in my vision, I managed to secure the necessary capital to breathe life into my dream project. But then again, there was no way my woes would disappear so quickly, for the bigger the aspiration, the greater the obstacles.

Right when structural, bureaucratic, and financial challenges had been taken care of, a new challenge arose—assembling the right team that would help me propel Lifespan to higher heights. In circumstances where real talent was scarce, finding truly talented candidates who had their hearts in the right place was even more challenging. From the start, I knew that I would not hire candidates merely based on their degrees or the university they had graduated from. To me, education and talent have always been concepts extending beyond certificates and records; I would rather recruit a bright, hardworking fresher with a ceaseless hunger for growth and learning than a top-ranking graduate who excels only in theoretical skills and not practical ones. Finding individuals who shared my passion and dedication while possessing integrity and humility was like searching for a needle in a haystack. Yet, through an exhaustive recruitment process, I managed to gather a team of like-minded people who believed in my vision for Lifespan as much as I did. As I have mentioned, a significant chunk of them is still with me, and having risen in rank and respect, they have been helping Lifespan prosper throughout these years.

Last but not least, operational challenges further tested my mettle as I grappled with the daunting task of selecting the right machinery and equipment for the manufacturing units of Lifespan. With a myriad of options available both domestically and internationally, each machine boasting different functions and capabilities, I was left feeling overwhelmed and uncertain. However, thanks to meticulous research and consultation with industry experts, I finally managed to procure the equipment best suited to meet the demands and standards of the state-of-the-art manufacturing units.

It may appear to some folks that the massive success that Lifespan has garnered is due to a favorable turn in fortune or just a gift from the universe. But honestly, it took me years of solid effort, difficult sacrifices, and unbeatable discipline as a one-person army to take my passion project to its current heights. The challenges I encountered during the whole process of establishment from start to finish would have rattled anyone else enough for them to quit midway without a second thought. I, though, fought lengthy legal battles, managed multiple aspects of business all by myself, and even participated in constructing the facilities from scratch. Besides, various factors come into play when starting an organization like Lifespan: inventory management, automation, increasing efficiency, risk mitigation, etc. I managed all these aspects majorly by myself and sometimes with valuable assistance from a small but solid team.

Thus, as is evident from the journey recounted, establishing the groundwork for Lifespan's triumph was far from effortless. I embraced every formidable challenge that came my way, boldly venturing into the nutraceuticals manufacturing sector. All my efforts were fueled by self-belief and unshakable faith in the transformative potential of the healthcare industry for our nation's future. My path was littered with sacrifices and hurdles, but all these sacrifices bore fruit, and all hurdles eventually turned into stepping stones toward success. Such is the power of determination and a powerful vision.

Life, the Greatest Teacher

At this point, having read about all that I have established and accomplished, you must be wondering if there is any straightforward formula for achieving multiple milestones in one's professional or entrepreneurial journey. Surely, there must be a secret sauce to my success that I am keeping a secret, right? You will be surprised to know that there is no secret sauce, only a deep willingness to learn from life as it comes. Now that I have shared my journey with you, dear reader, I want you to know some things that will significantly help you throughout your life. I thus present to you what I have learned from my life, 'My Advice 101!'

First, always know who to have on your team and, more importantly, assign the right person to the right job. I have always had the knack for selecting the best people who I know for a fact will always be on my side and help me expand my Business and Vision. In fact, when hiring the staff for Lifespan, I didn't focus only on candidates' educational backgrounds. Having been a backbencher at one point, I knew that hard work and dedication can always beat talent. Also, to me, a person's integrity and eagerness to improve trump the importance of the name of the institute from which they've graduated. So, I ensured I hired people I knew would make my mission and vision their own and stay with Lifespan for years. Now, and I am not joking when I say this, 90% of the people I had brought into my business as interns now have managerial positions and supervise entire departments. Even most of those recruited into my other ventures as trainees in 2006 are still with me, helping me propel those ventures to higher heights. Such is the effect of choosing the right people on your team.

I am also drawn to those who view themselves as students of life, for life, because I am one such person. Back when I didn't even remotely know anything about the health and wellness sector, I made sure I didn't pigeonhole myself into a particular niche I was comfortable with; I always chose discomfort over complacency. As you can see, this frame of mind can get you to places in life you would have never imagined you'd be in. Never stop being curious;

never let anyone discourage you from giving your best to whatever you wish to pursue. Always be hungry for more.

Secondly, with each rung on the ladder of success you climb, pull some others up with you. If not for the benevolence of our support networks and all the communities involved in turning our visions into reality, none of us would have reached where we are. Thus, it is always essential to give back to where we came from, and Lifespan has been doing a swell job with that. For every product sold at Lifespan, we created jobs for hundreds of vendors and a stable income source for their families. We also plan to recruit at least 1000 farmers nationwide to support our expansion plans. This way, with just one idea, we ended up creating new lives for many others, and we will continue to do so for as long as possible.

Finally, an essential thing to remember is to have a passion outside your profession that makes you happy at the end of a busy day. I have always loved the sport of cricket to bits, so I took that love to a new level and bought a stake in the cricket team, the Vizag Warriors. I also recently took up yoga to improve my health through physical exercise and spiritual alignment, and I've been loving every minute of it. The time I take off from work helps me recalibrate myself for whatever life has to offer me every day, and that is what you should also do.

I guarantee that following these practices will help you create a beautiful and fulfilling life for yourself while you chase your dreams with full gusto.

Ultimately, I plan to devote myself to the betterment of humankind, one country at a time, and to do whatever it takes to help create better lives worldwide. I am proud of myself and hopeful for all the accolades I must collect. It will be a long and tedious path, but I bet I will make it through every examination with flying colors, for where there is a will, there is a way.

This is the story of "how I did it," dear reader! If I could, so can you!

AUTHOR BIO

Narendra Ram's journey from an HR trainee to a thriving entrepreneur is a testament to strategic vision, exceptional interpersonal skills and unwavering commitment. As a first-generation business owner, his impact extends far beyond the corporate world, shapingsuccess stories and touching lives with innovation, leadership and positive change. In his own words, "My career plan was to start my own business, and I've always been drawn to health and wellness"; starting a business demands passion, determination and resilience.

His passion for sports and health consciousness resulted the inception of Lifespan, a world class manufacturing facility crafted for health and wellness products. The aim of Lifespan was providing high-quality food supplements to promote daily health and well-being of individuals. His personal commitment to a healthy lifestyle became the cornerstone of Lifespan's mission to offer nutritional supplements, Ayurvedic and herbal products of the highest quality.

Narendra Ram's influence extends beyond Lifespan. He has ventured into various sectors,founding Lifespan Pharmacies to ensure universal access to essential medications and Lifespan Super Specialty Hospitals, where innovation meets healing to create a healthier future for all. His dedication to promoting good health led to the establishment of N Sports, a sports company that invests in major leagues in India and supports emerging athletes, nurturing them from national to global success.

Driven by a desire to give back to society, Narendra Ram also founded Feel Foundation, a determined NGO dedicated to enhancing the quality of life for underprivileged children through education and healthcare initiatives.

Narendra Ram embodies the qualities of a visionary leader—demanding yet compassionate,generous and considerate. He believes in the power of empathy to drive positive change and tirelessly works towards improving the lives of others, both through his business ventures and philanthropic endeavors.

His legacy is one of kindness, generosity and advocacy for humanitarian causes, inspiring others to make a difference and leave a lasting impact on the world

NARENDRA RAM, CO-AUTHOR

3

UNLOCKING POTENTIAL: THE PATH TO EFFECTIVE LEADERSHIP

BY

ANU WAKHLU

"You cannot mandate productivity; you must provide the tools to let people become their best."

– Steve Jobs

As Steve Jobs emphasized, productivity can't be mandated; people must be equipped with the right tools and resources to unleash their best. This principle lay at the core of Pragati Leadership's inception. Taking a stroll back to the early 80s, the HR landscape was a stark contrast from today. People were often regarded as mere resources relegated to output and tasks.

Revisiting this era a quarter-century ago, HR was still finding its footing, primarily centered on Industrial Relations (IR) and personnel administration. The term 'human resources' had yet to gain prevalence, with the strategic potential of HR in its infancy.

Over the past 40 years, however, HR has undergone a remarkable transformation.

No longer confined to paperwork and personnel matters, HR has evolved into a strategic partner, collaborating closely with thought leaders to align human capital strategies with organizational goals. From recruiting and developing talent to fostering a positive workplace culture, HR plays a pivotal role in driving business success.

At Pragati Leadership, our primary focus has always been on the dynamic space of leadership development. While the HR landscape evolved, we carved our niche, immersing ourselves in this transformative journey. Modern HR extends far beyond traditional functions, actively engaging in creating a positive employee environment and experience. Leveraging technological advancements, tools like applicant tracking systems, HRIS, and performance management streamline processes, promoting efficiency.

Continuous learning and development have been integral to our mandate. Our dedicated professionals design and implement training programs aligned with business objectives, ensuring that our team possesses the skills and knowledge needed for success. This evolution reflects a dynamic and responsive function that adapts to the changing needs of the workforce and business environment.

In today's scenario, where organizations prioritize their people, HR stands central in shaping the future of work. However, this was a far cry from the reality about 35-40 years ago. This journey signifies the significant transformation within the HR landscape, and at Pragati Leadership, we continue to stride forward, dedicated to empowering individuals and organizations through leadership development.

In the leadership development journey, Human Resources (HR) emerges as a crucial ally, weaving a strategic partnership with organizational leaders to seamlessly integrate training endeavors with overarching business objectives. At Pragati Leadership, we recognize the pivotal role played by HR in identifying leadership gaps, crafting customized training programs, and diligently assessing their impact. This collaborative approach ensures a steady stream of capable leaders, fortified by succession planning to address any shifts in leadership dynamics.

Moreover, HR's influence extends to fostering a culture of continuous learning within our organization. Through initiatives championing diversity, inclusion, and employee engagement, HR at Pragati Leadership contributes to forming a resilient leadership team. Our commitment to cultivating visionary leaders is embodied in HR's dedication to aligning organizational strategies, thereby ensuring a robust leadership pipeline capable of navigating the ever-evolving landscapes of the business world.

But let me start at the very beginning—a very good place to start. When you read, you begin with A-B-C; when you sing, you begin with Do-Re-Mi. But when you are a fresh, first-gen entrepreneur, where do you begin?

Over the past three decades, Pragati has worked closely with more than 300 multinational companies and various firms that turn to us for leadership consulting. It's been a journey, and I've reached a point where things are going well, but it wasn't always like this.

Before conceiving Pragati Leadership, my husband navigated his role at Tata Motors, and I was partly committed to their CSR department (I had a part-time job in the Tata Motors CSR department). Life was well. Well, it was pretty routine, quite "normal."

Our days were well-structured, and life seemed to dance along a rhythmically predictable path. Yet, within the cadence of the seemingly ordinary, the seeds of something truly extraordinary quietly germinated.

This narrative of transformation commenced its vibrant overture in the lively city of Jamshedpur, where I assumed my part-time role at Tata Motors during the 80s.

Amid this orchestrated routine, a resolute desire began to swell within me—a yearning to transcend corporate boundaries and weave a tapestry of positive change. Whether it be in the nuanced art of management or in the empowering embrace of women's narratives, I felt the call to make a difference. The catalyst for this change, no matter how modest its inception, marked a poignant turning point. The ignition was purely intrinsic, a flame stoked by a personal zeal to be a harbinger of change. Reflecting on that initial push, I am grateful, for it set the stage for my current role as a fervent advocate for women's leadership.

During my part-time tenure with Tata Motors, which unfolded against the backdrop of the 80s, I embarked on an unconventional journey that sought to contest prevalent norms surrounding women's roles in the workplace. It was a period marked by gender biases and a societal landscape where women were often marginalized in professional spheres.

I initiated workshops with educators and teachers, focusing on the art of making teaching a joyful experience. Simultaneously, I also extended my reach to NGO leaders, imparting insights on managerial excellence. As I delved into these sessions, the realization dawned that the pursuit of knowledge and empowerment was not confined to the boardrooms and classrooms alone.

Amidst these educational crescendos, a profound realization began to crystallize—an epiphany that transcended the hallowed halls of boardrooms and classrooms. The pursuit of knowledge and empowerment, I discovered, was not constrained by the physical boundaries of a corporate office or a classroom setting. It was a universal force that had the potential to uplift and transform lives, regardless of the societal compartments that sought to confine it.

This period of my life, set against the societal backdrop of gender biases, was a testament to the transformative power of education and empowerment. It was an era where, despite societal constraints, I dared to challenge the narrative and contribute to the paradigm shift that paved the way for more inclusive and empowered workplaces. The echoes of those workshops and insights continue to resonate, serving as beacons of inspiration for those who dare to defy limitations and strive for excellence.

In a whimsical turn during the early '80s, I found myself navigating societal currents where women were not prevalent in the corporate workforce, rooted in deep-seated traditional gender roles that often made the corporate world elusive for women.

Amid formidable barriers for women in careers and entrepreneurship, I started taking Kashmiri cooking lessons for homemakers in Jamshedpur. The introduction of Kashmiri Cooking classes in the early '80s emerged as a unique platform for the Jamshedpuri women to transcend traditional roles. This novel venture provided homemakers with an escape from conventional culinary practices, inviting them to explore exotic Kashmiri flavors and fostering camaraderie. The initiative, akin to inviting frogs in a pond to explore beyond their familiar surroundings, enriched their skills and became a catalyst for cultural exchange. This metaphorical departure from their pond added a vibrant thread to the cultural fabric of our stint in Jamshedpur.

Beyond being culinary tutorials, these classes transformed into sanctuaries of empowerment, breaking stereotypes and fostering a sense of community. Against the backdrop of societal change, the kitchen evolved from a confined space to a realm of possibility and self-discovery. Retrospectively, these classes played a vital role in preserving Kashmiri heritage and reshaping narratives around women's roles, displaying the transformative power of education, even when served in the form of a delectable Kashmiri dish.

As I write this, I'm taken back in time to when a heart-warming interlude emerged in my cooking classes. As the aroma of spices lingered, my eager kids and our loyal dog gathered, tongues hanging in anticipation, plates ready. Their excitement mirrored the joy of exploration. In these kitchen moments, the boundaries between teacher and learners blurred. The act of sharing food became a metaphor for sharing knowledge, breaking barriers, and fostering community. It was a simple yet profound reminder that the joy of learning transcends generations. Amidst the clatter of plates and the laughter of children, the story of empowerment and education continued to unfold—a delightful residue of culinary exploration.

This era of multi-faceted engagement was the intersection of passion, purpose, and societal impact. It instilled confidence in me and laid the foundation for what would eventually evolve into Pragati Leadership—a symphony of transformative leadership. The journey from the meticulously choreographed routines of the corporate world to the diverse landscapes of education, empowerment, and culinary exploration became a pivotal chapter in my personal and professional crescendo. Little did we know that those seemingly routine days were nurturing the seeds of an organization committed to holistic leadership development and positive societal impact. The journey from the corridors of Tata Motors to the heart-warming scenes of shared meals with our eager kids and a delighted dog became a pivotal chapter in our story of growth and transformation.

The regular 9-to-5 routine? It was a familiar territory. But we wanted to spice things up a bit. That's when we decided to move from Jamshedpur to Pune, where my husband sought to grow his career with a stint at a Management Consulting firm. A solid plan, right? Well, not quite. Just as we had started to settle into the groove, tragedy struck—the company's founder unfortunately passed away. The passing of the founder was both disheartening and unexpected, occurring within the initial six months of our relocation to Pune.

Suddenly, we stood at a crossroads. It was time to make a decision. A life-altering decision that would affect our entire future. To jump into another corporate gig or to take a leap of faith and start our very own venture. The unexpected turn of events forced us to confront the stark choice between the safety of the familiar and the allure of the unknown.

Emerging from a middle-class background where the daily rhythm revolved around the predictability of a 9-to-5 job, the prospect of delving into entrepreneurship posed a considerable challenge. While I had been exploring consulting, a realization dawned upon both my husband and me—we were parents to very young children, and the security of a traditional white-collar job eluded both of us.

This decision added an extra layer of complexity, marked by the presence of our two little ones, a lack of financial security, and a family history deeply intertwined with the stability of salaried positions. The initiation of our entrepreneurial journey became more than a career shift; it evolved into a leap of faith, a courageous stride into uncharted territories.

As challenging as it was for us, it was time to decide. The genesis of our journey, however, was marked by a specific moment of realization or maybe a profound shift in our perspectives. Our pivotal moment came in '88 when we recognized that the traditional work environments were not fully utilizing employees' potential. Employers were unable to recognize the untapped possibilities fully within the prevailing work culture. Having also worked at big corporations, we realized that it was evident that the full potential of employees was not being harnessed in the prevailing work culture.

In particular, the focus on technical training was restrictive, solely emphasizing the completion of tasks without considering personal development.

It felt as though we were there merely to fulfill a job description. This realization became a catalyst for change in today's evolving environment.

The transformation was not just about doing a job; it was a paradigm shift towards realizing our own potential and contributing to a larger purpose. We aimed to go beyond the routine and ensure that everything we did enhanced our surroundings. It marked a departure from the conventional job mindset, where personal development and larger contributions were often overlooked.

Realizing that a company like ours could bridge a critical gap for businesses globally pushed us to venture into these uncharted terrains. We found ourselves unable to pursue our true passion in a job— you know we wanted to educate, consult, and empower individuals within corporations to run their businesses in a holistic and humane way. The roles we previously occupied lacked the scope for these endeavors, catalyzing our entrepreneurial spark. This realization became the spark that ignited our entrepreneurial venture—a venture fueled by the belief that the traditional employer-employee dynamic needed a transformative overhaul. The little bit of consultancy I had dabbled in and the demise of our new employer further intensified this realization, ultimately propelling us into our very own entrepreneurial venture.

The shift from a service-oriented background to assuming the responsibility of delivering these services to corporations occurred when we noticed that all of HR was not conducive to employees. They were being treated more like checkbox fillers on the employer's to-do list, focusing solely on cranking up the output.

I believe 'recognizing something is a problem is half the battle won.' We identified a gap in the prevalent working environment of the time. But starting out, we initially had a separate set of challenges to overcome.

The challenges we faced hereafter reached beyond the entrepreneurial world. They permeated into the very fabric of our familial life, demanding a delicate balance between sustaining our household, managing everyday expenses, and reshaping our lifestyle to harmonize with the demands of entrepreneurship. It was a holistic transformation, requiring not only professional adaptability but also a fundamental shift in our approach to family dynamics and financial stability. This endeavor tested our resilience and commitment, urging us to redefine our understanding of success and security in the pursuit of our entrepreneurial dreams. It was a thrilling yet unpredictable period, where every step into the unknown held the potential to shape our destiny.

In the nascent stages of our entrepreneurial venture, the hurdles were not just hurdles—they were formidable mountains. Securing appointments proved to be a formidable challenge, amplified by our status as newcomers to the city, lacking any established connections. Undeterred, we adopted a hands-on approach, eagerly embracing any assignment that crossed our path. This translated into a dynamic routine of multi-scaling, burning the midnight oil, and, perhaps most importantly, a humble willingness to shelve our egos in order to meet the varied demands of our diverse clientele.

Amidst the relentless grind, a glimmer of success emerged, accompanied by a modest degree of recognition. Yet, this newfound ease was not a harbinger of smooth sailing. As our entrepreneurial endeavors gained traction, a fresh set of challenges unfolded. The focal point shifted from our individual grind to team dynamics, ushering in the era of retention struggles. The transition from solo entrepreneurs to team leaders necessitated a reevaluation of roles and responsibilities.

Embarking on our entrepreneurial journey, the absence of a dedicated team prompted me to shoulder a myriad of roles, ranging from co-founder to typist, telephone operator, accountant, and content creator. Just imagine, a young mother, trying to cook and keep the baby from crying, while the phone rings, it could be a potential client or a client calling for updates. Navigating these phone calls with clients in a professional manner became quite the balancing act when the pressure cooker would decide that it's time for it to make its presence known, accompanied by the symphony of a wailing child on the sidelines. This diverse engagement stemmed from a response to necessity. The dynamic nature of a startup demanded a hands-on approach, where understanding and performing every facet of the business, as well as our familial ties, became crucial for survival.

As our venture gained momentum and a team gradually took shape, transitioning from solo entrepreneurship to collaborative team dynamics marked a significant shift. Roles that I once managed single-handedly found their match as dedicated individuals assumed specific responsibilities within the team. This transformation streamlined operations, allowing each team member to excel in their specialized domain.

However, this journey posed its challenges, shedding light on the intricacies of team dynamics and the balance between individual versatility and cohesive teamwork. Team dynamics often trap individuals in crafted roles, emphasizing do's and don'ts. The shift towards specialist roles rather than generic positions brought about a new set of challenges, especially concerning people's career aspirations.

For instance, individuals in professional settings often grapple with career goals, a concern less pronounced in the entrepreneurial solo space. Moreover, as a company grows, the transition from a cohesive, informal network to professional standards becomes inevitable. Maintaining an informal yet professional atmosphere can be challenging but remains crucial for fostering a culture where relationships flourish.

Navigating these challenges in team dynamics and retention became a crucible that forged our entrepreneurial spirit. Learning from diverse roles and witnessing the emergence of specialized team positions highlighted the delicate interplay between individual versatility and cohesive teamwork. This journey underscored the importance of evolving roles—from a solo endeavor to a collaborative team effort—establishing a robust foundation for the ongoing success of our entrepreneurial venture.

In 1988, my husband Arun and I embarked on establishing Pragati Leadership, driven by a vision that challenged the prevailing industry norm of viewing individuals merely as resources for output or task completion. Our radical vision aimed to create work environments and organizations that genuinely inspire individuals to unfold their innate potential in their professional pursuits. When Arun and I founded Pragati Leadership, we defied the prevailing industry mindset, daring to see individuals not merely as resources for output but as beings with untapped potential. Our vision was to envision work environments that empower personal growth.

Over the course of our journey, there has been a constant evolution in our methodology—a meticulous refinement of our approach. Our pursuit revolves around striking a delicate balance between unleashing the latent potential residing within individuals and leveraging management principles such as procedures, practices, models, and tools. As founders, Arun and I have been privileged to engage with top management, contributing our expertise to shape or reshape organizational DNA and build leadership talent. This intricate process is not a one-time effort but an ongoing journey, a continuous endeavor that embodies our unwavering commitment to transformative leadership.

Our driving force is a genuine aspiration to redefine leadership development, to transcend conventional boundaries and pave the way for a new era of empowered and visionary leaders. At the core of our approach is the profound recognition that every business possesses a distinct mission and vision. We, as facilitators, remain attuned to the unique essence of each enterprise, acknowledging the inherent humanity that binds us in our shared pursuit.

So, what is our mission? It goes beyond merely unlocking people's inner potential. Our mission includes equipping these people (leaders) with tools that amplify effectiveness. Focused on fostering a 'I can, I will' culture, we empower individuals while providing tools and competencies to enhance proficiency. Our approach integrates a holistic array of models, practices, and competencies, nurturing individual growth and collective productivity. Centered around delivering impactful, tailor-made learning solutions, our mission prioritizes sustainable breakthrough results and the well-being of individuals. Guided by core values like Self-mastery, Integrity, Customer Centricity, Passionate Ownership, and Collaboration, we design diverse learning journeys, spanning from Strategic Leadership to Inspirational Leadership.

In navigating this intricate balance, we recognize that true empowerment lies at the intersection of unlocking potential and providing the means to manifest that potential. This reframing not only clarifies our mission but also underscores the multifaceted nature of our commitment to fostering transformative leadership.

Today, HR practices have evolved significantly, moving beyond viewing individuals as mere productivity tools. Employees are acknowledged for their integral role in shaping the organization's identity, acting as brand ambassadors and engagement champions that influence workplace culture.

The evolution doesn't stop there. In the earlier HR era, the focus was predominantly on work-related competencies—a narrow lens that has since broadened significantly. The contemporary HR landscape takes a holistic view of individuals, acknowledging their multifaceted roles in society, family, and the environment. I also observed a particularly refreshing transformation occurring in the demographics of decision-making. The once-prevailing image of middle-aged white-haired men at the helm has given way to a diverse mix of decision-makers. In this modern HR era, the voice of a dynamic 25-year-old carries as much weight as any other, signaling the demystification of hierarchy, gender roles, and power equations. Today, a diverse mix includes the young and spirited, contributing to decision-making, resulting in a refreshing demystification of traditional hierarchies, gender roles, and power dynamics. This shift has ushered in a more inclusive and dynamic decision-making environment, injecting vitality and diversity into organizational leadership.

In my early thirties, my first training program unfolded in a room filled with middle-aged men, marking a distinctive moment in my professional journey. The stark contrast in reception became immediately apparent, with challenges surfacing due to the unfamiliarity of having a woman as their trainer. Fast forward to the present, and the landscape has undergone a transformative shift, reflecting positive strides in fostering gender inclusivity. The journey from those early sessions, characterized by skepticism and resistance, to the current scenario, where the presence of women in such roles is met with greater openness, highlights the progress in societal attitudes and the resilience required to navigate traditionally male-centric spaces.

Amidst the changing tides of acceptability in professional settings, my journey took on a more purpose-driven trajectory. The initial challenges I faced as a woman trainer fueled a deep-seated passion for advocating women's presence in decision-making roles and fostering a holistic approach to management and leadership.

My commitment to women's leadership arises from the belief that gender diversity enhances decision-making. Recognizing the importance of amplifying women's voices, I've dedicated two decades to designing and conducting workshops tailored for women. These sessions go beyond conventional professional development, providing platforms to empower women in overcoming societal pressures and internal doubts. Emphasizing the significance of breaking free from external expectations, the workshops foster self-confidence and equip women to navigate the professional landscape with resilience.

In alignment with these endeavors, along with a close friend, I am currently channeling my experiences, insights, and advocacy into a significant project—a co-authored book on Women's Leadership. This upcoming publication aims to encapsulate the essence of women's empowerment in leadership roles. In weaving together the narrative of my professional journey, from navigating the challenges of being a woman in training sessions to advocating and being a part of women's leadership, the underlying theme remains consistent: the pursuit of inclusivity, empowerment, and a more equitable professional landscape.

The journey from a room of skeptical middle-aged men to advocating for women's voices and leadership roles epitomizes the transformative power of resilience, passion, and an unwavering commitment to fostering positive change.

Throughout the initial stages of my journey, undoubtedly, doubts crept in. The absence of incoming orders for our services triggered fleeting thoughts about the security of a conventional job. However, these doubts were short-lived. The vision we harbored, coupled with the drive to create an impact, fueled our determination. Doubts, while natural, yielded to the unwavering belief that our aspirations were not only achievable but also held the potential for significant impact.

On this transformative journey, mentors played a pivotal role in shaping our path. Their guidance and support, often from experienced business figures, were instrumental in navigating the nuances of entrepreneurship. These mentors, drawn to the work we were passionate about, generously shared their time, offering invaluable insights on business building, potential obstacles, and even providing access to essential networks.

Among the nuggets of wisdom we received, one particularly invaluable piece of advice stood out—cultivate relationships with the personal secretaries of Managing Directors. This strategic counsel emphasized the enduring nature of such relationships, transcending potential changes in leadership. A good equation with personal secretaries, we were advised, could pave the way for valuable facetime with their senior executives.

The moment of full commitment materialized when we had the company letterheads in hand. It symbolized a point of no return, a commitment to the path we had chosen. From that moment, there was no looking back.

The journey, like any entrepreneurial endeavor, commenced with its set of challenges. Introducing our offerings to a new market, garnering trust, credibility, and making sales for intangible products like behavioral and leadership training posed significant hurdles. However, persistence became our ally. We focused on building relationships with clients, consistently delivering excellence, and going the extra mile to accommodate their needs. Overcoming these initial challenges laid the foundation for Pragati Leadership's ethos of commitment, resilience, and client-centric excellence.

Upon reaching our significant milestones, the concept of returning to an "ordinary world" takes on a different hue. Instead of reverting to a previous normal, we find ourselves embracing the behaviors and actions that led to our success, effectively establishing a new normal. This shift becomes a permanent feature of our journey. The practices and strategies that propelled us toward our goals don't fade into the background; they become integral to our ongoing operations. Rather than a descent into the old normal, it's a continuous journey forward, maintaining and evolving the new normal until the next set of challenges and goals present themselves. This perspective encapsulates the essence of perpetual growth and adaptation inherent in the entrepreneurial journey.

Navigating the challenges posed by the Covid phase emerged as a critical juncture in our journey. As a company deeply engaged in face-to-face coaching and training, the sudden imposition of lockdowns and restrictions dealt a severe blow to our regular operations. Adapting swiftly, we honed our skills for online sessions and diligently worked on building credibility in the digital realm. The initial excitement and exhilaration of facing this challenge head-on were palpable. Notably, we took pride in being one of the rare companies that did not resort to employee layoffs during this tumultuous period. Instead, we redirected our focus toward re-skilling and enhancing our organizational capacities.

However, in the entrepreneurial realm, moments of reprieve or reward are fleeting. While there is a sense of gratification in successfully navigating a tough period, it's quite momentary. The relentless nature of entrepreneurship ensures that the fleeting moments of accomplishment are swiftly replaced by the anticipation of the next challenge. This perpetual cycle keeps us on our toes, fostering an environment of continuous growth and adaptation.

As my journey unfolds, I find myself still immersed in the ongoing pursuit of our vision, recognizing that the path ahead is vast and filled with challenges. Amidst this continuous journey, several lessons have become apparent, shaping both my professional and personal outlook.

I still vividly recall the pivotal moment when our steadfast dedication and refusal to veer off course led us to secure our very first assignment. This initial milestone at PLI marked a significant turning point—a substantial order for 500 books focusing on Time Management and Planners.
Ah, the memory is still crystal clear.

The gravity of this project spurred each member of the PLI team into action, igniting a collective effort that extended into late hours. Despite the challenges and the demands placed upon us, our commitment remained unwavering. It was not merely about meeting a demand; it was a testament to our shared commitment to excellence and the fulfillment of our client's needs. The late nights were not just hours on the clock; they were a manifestation of our dedication and the resilience that defined our journey from the inception of PLI.

Here's the kicker—the entire PLI squad rolled up their sleeves and dived headfirst into the task, burning the midnight oil to meet the demands of this colossal endeavor. Late nights weren't just hours on the clock; they were a symphony of commitment and a testament to our relentless pursuit of excellence. It wasn't just about fulfilling an order; it was our dreams, dedication, and resilience that had started to take shape.

From our day one up to the present moment, our mentors have been a steadfast source of support. Even when their physical presence was not feasible, their words have echoed with us, guiding us every step along the way. Let me impart some of our collective learnings to all aspiring entrepreneurs.

First and foremost, mastery of one's subject or area of work emerges as an indispensable aspect of the entrepreneurial journey. There are no shortcuts; investing time and effort in mastering the craft is non-negotiable.

Secondly, authenticity proves to be a guiding light. Fearlessness and courage, rooted in being one's authentic self, create a unique narrative that resonates with others. The authenticity of character and purpose allows us to navigate challenges with integrity, fostering genuine connections and trust. Remaining true to oneself, even in the face of adversity, becomes a beacon illuminating the path forward.

Additionally, maintaining practices that foster centeredness and grounding serves as a compass, ensuring a steady course through the dynamic and unpredictable entrepreneurial landscape. To navigate the complexities of our journey, adopting practices that promote centeredness and grounding becomes crucial.

The ebb and flow of challenges and triumphs can be emotionally charged, making it essential to have rituals or habits that bring balance and perspective. These practices serve as anchors, keeping us rooted and resilient in the face of dynamic circumstances.

Reflecting on how this journey has changed me, I recognize a transformation towards increased patience, openness to possibilities, and heightened awareness of opportunities. The professional dimensions of my work have transcended into personal realms, influencing how I approach life beyond the professional sphere.

Professionally, my endeavors have gravitated towards a distinctive niche that I am genuinely passionate about—organizational culture and purpose. My fervor lies in shaping work environments, modes of operation, and thought processes that contribute to a thriving culture. It's a sphere where my organization, as well as myself, have made a substantial impact, carving out a distinctive space within this domain.

Another large area of interest is coaching. So, a little trivia about me. I currently hold the coveted title of a Master Certified Coach from ICF. It is a certification achieved by a select few; it reflects not only a commitment to the craft but also the proficiency and depth with which the coach approaches coaching. With less than 50 such certified individuals in India, this achievement stands as a testament of the dedication to the art and science of coaching.

A noteworthy area of focus is the development of women as leaders. While I may not definitively claim widespread recognition for this yet, it's an area that holds deep personal significance. Working towards creating avenues for women to ascend into decision-making positions, I am committed to fostering a more inclusive and humane work environment.

Currently, I am authoring a book on this very subject, aiming to provide insights and guidance on how women can navigate their way into leadership roles and positions of influence. This endeavor aligns with my belief that a greater presence of women in leadership positions contributes to a more humanistic and compassionate approach to work.

I love it and absolutely thrive when tackling complex challenges that lack a straightforward answer, when problem-solving for my clients. My expertise shines in scenarios where clients seek solutions to building and nurturing women leaders for the future, retaining women within their organizations, or creating a winning culture conducive to productivity and making their workplace a desirable haven. I relish the opportunity to craft frameworks and architectures tailored to address specific needs, especially when clients present their goals without prescribing a rigid script. The collaborative process involves consultations and discussions to fine-tune the approach.

Over the course of my career, I have collaborated with notable corporations in the B2B space, including but not limited to Sudarshan Chemicals, Atlas Copco, Honeywell, Aurobindo Pharma, BASF, BMC, etc. My engagements with these organizations have spanned various facets, from developing leadership programs and learning architectures to enhancing their employer brand, making them attractive to potential hires. These projects aimed to maximize return on investment and strategically position these companies in the competitive market.

However, I contend that maintaining a work-life balance is a skill that evolves over time. In the initial phases of building the organization, work often consumed a significant portion of my time, a common experience for many entrepreneurs. An amusing incident occurred when my daughters, observing my busy schedule, playfully dubbed our home a guest house, prompting moments of reflection.

As the organization matured, a conscious decision was made to limit work hours to six per day. This deliberate choice allows for a step back, providing time to unwind and indulge in personal interests like gardening, hiking, writing, poetry, culinary pursuits, and my love for animals. The separation of professional and personal life has become a well-honed skill, emphasizing that work is a support system for life, not the other way around.

Delegating responsibilities and trusting the capable team we've built have been crucial. While not every assignment is flawless, creating an environment where team members can contribute authentically outweighs occasional missteps. It's a journey of reframing the approach to work, focusing on enabling the team to thrive collectively, trusting others, and striking a balance that nurtures both personal and professional aspects.

The luxury of choosing time commitments adds an extra layer of support.

During leisure moments, I indulge in various activities, from strolling with my dog and hosting gatherings to writing, flower arranging, and occasional feet-up relaxation. This intentional shift from work's cognitive demands to hands-on pursuits serves as a counterbalance, engaging my right brain and offering respite from professional challenges.

Motivation for my professional endeavors stems from intrinsic sources. With a self-motivated disposition, I find satisfaction in the work's quality and the opportunity to explore new challenges.

While external validation is appreciated, the driving force remains the intrinsic motivation to innovate, explore, and contribute meaningfully to clients' needs.

A steadfast belief in each day offering new opportunities, combined with feeling wanted by clients and being entrusted with diverse assignments, fuels my motivation. In a saturated industry, authenticity, sustained interest in the work, and a commitment to continuous learning form the pillars supporting my professional drive.

Learning, for me, is an ongoing process. Enrolling in formal courses, acquiring new skills, and seeking personal growth through activities like whiplash, treks, or courses on creative thinking contribute to my engagement with life. Embracing the philosophy that age should never limit one's potential, I strive to stay motivated by embracing new challenges, staying authentic, and continually investing in personal and professional growth.

Recognizing that not everyone shares my intrinsic motivation, I consciously tailor my approach to acknowledge and appreciate diverse working styles. While I may not seek external motivation, I understand its significance for others, fostering positive strokes and acknowledgment where needed.

Apart from corporate collaborations, our commitment extends to the social sector. As an Ashoka Fellow, I operate as a social innovator, contributing to the development of the social space. Our NGO initiatives focus on leadership development, learning program implementation, and strategic guidance for organizations within the social sector. Active participation in women's networks further amplifies our impact, fostering a more inclusive and empowered community.

But that's not all—my journey has been graced with several accolades, each a reflection of my commitment to excellence and contribution to society:

Exceptional Woman of Excellence Award: Presented by the World Economic Forum and ALL Ladies League on 8 March 2018 at The Hague.

- Grassroots Woman of the Decade Award: Conferred by ALL Ladies League of ASSOCHAM in 2014.
- Rotary GSE Award: Acknowledging my representation of India in Austria and Germany.
- Fellowship for NGO Leader: Received in the USA, further solidifying my commitment to impactful leadership.

These accolades not only celebrate past achievements but also fuel my ongoing dedication to creating meaningful change and contributing to the fields of coaching and social entrepreneurship.

My work encompasses a spectrum of activities, ranging from leadership development to organizational culture enhancement, consistently delivering tailored solutions to meet the unique needs of our diverse clientele.

My life outside the professional sphere is a harmonious blend of diverse activities, providing balance and inspiration for each workday. Contributing to meaningful causes is a significant part of my journey. The Pragati Foundation, our NGO focused on sustainable livelihoods for young people, goes beyond charity—it's a commitment to creating lasting impacts.

Soroptimist International, a global organization dedicated to women and children's well-being, holds a special place in my heart.

Serving as the national president for India and Pune adds depth to my philanthropic journey.

Additionally, my passion for providing safe homes for stray dogs reflects a personal commitment to compassion in action.

These activities transcend mere checkboxes; they signify a dedication to the broader societal canvas. Originating from social and community work, my professional trajectory into the corporate realm hasn't altered my commitment to causes that matter. It's about crafting a tapestry of positive change, one endeavor at a time.

Pragati Leadership embraces the Quadruple Bottom Line, focusing on Purpose, People, Planet, and Profit. Our philosophy transcends conventional metrics, integrating psychological insights, values, and methodical thinking into leadership interventions. With a vision of fostering "One Wholesome World," we strive to catalyze a global movement towards wholesomeness, ensuring fulfilling lives for all beings.

As a beacon of transformative leadership, Pragati Leadership not only shapes successful organizations but also inspires leaders grounded in holistic principles. Rooted in a rich history, impactful philosophy, and a dedicated team, we continue to shape the leadership development landscape through our unique and holistic approach.

Our multidimensional approach covers strategic leadership, collaboration, growth strategy, culture transformation, and inspirational leadership. We empower leaders to envision, plan, lead, and implement strategies effectively, fostering a growth mindset for breakthrough results. Our interventions emphasize collaboration across teams, functions, or locations, delivering high-performance teams aligned with organizational goals.

In supporting organizations to achieve growth targets, we provide strategic direction, energize teams, and enable leaders to navigate within dynamic market conditions. Our diverse programs include strategic leadership, collaboration, growth strategy, culture transformation, inspirational leadership, management development, people management, competency-based training, execution excellence, and self-awareness.

Actively engaging in cultural transformation, we co-create or revisit vision, mission, and values, ensuring alignment across all organizational levels. Our interventions empower leaders to inspire and motivate teams, addressing aspects such as style, communication, executive presence, and emotional intelligence.

For those embarking on similar entrepreneurial journeys, as I have elaborated before, I would offer the following advice:

1. Master your subject/area of work. There can be no shortcuts to this.

2. Stay true to your authentic self; be fearless and courageous; be your own person.

3. Have practices that keep you centered and grounded.

As I reflect on the collective journey we've undertaken, a tapestry emerges woven with invaluable lessons and principles that have become the guiding light for our endeavors. The ongoing nature of this expedition toward our vision prompts me to share a distilled essence that encapsulates the ethos of our approach.

The pivotal lesson underscores the importance of mastering our subject, emphasizing dedication and an unwavering commitment to excellence. Authenticity serves as another cornerstone, distinguishing us in a competitive industry, as it stands testament to the power of individuality. The third guiding principle emphasizes building powerful networks, recognizing the significance of meaningful connections that extend beyond transactions, fostering a shared journey of growth, guidance, and opportunities.

Amidst the fervor of professional pursuits, the importance of maintaining a harmonious work-life balance becomes evident. Our journey is not merely about professional achievements; it encompasses the entirety of our lives. Striking this balance ensures that our professional commitments enhance rather than overshadow the myriad facets of our existence.

The principle of having fun and actively embracing the joy of learning encapsulates the spirit with which we navigate this expedition. In the dynamic landscape of our work, finding joy in the process, coupled with an unyielding commitment to continual learning, defines our approach.

I would love to sign off by saying that this ongoing journey is a tapestry interwoven with the threads of expertise, authenticity, meaningful connections, balanced living, and the sheer enjoyment of the path less traveled. As we continue to evolve and shape our narrative, these principles remain as guiding stars, illuminating not only the way forward but the essence of who we are and what we aspire to become.

AUTHOR BIO

Anu is a dynamic leader renowned for her contributions to leadership development, organizational change, and women's empowerment. As the author of "Time and Life Management" and Co-founder of Pragati Leadership, she's recognized for her ability to 'make things happen' with patience and perseverance. With expertise in organizational change and HR consultancy, Anu has transformed systems for leading manufacturing firms, earning them spots on the Great Place to Work list. As an Executive Coach, she has worked with companies like Siemens and Capgemini, and facilitated change for organizations worldwide.

Anu's impact extends globally, with assignments in locations from Dubai to Vietnam. Her academic background in nutrition and strategic management, coupled with accolades such as a Gold Medal for her MSC, attest to her remarkable journey of empowering individuals and organizations alike. An Ashoka Fellow, Anu has led initiatives in women's health and NGO capacity building, alongside her role as President Elect of Soroptomist International. Beyond her professional endeavors, she finds joy in sketching, painting, and nature walks with her dog, Zorba.

ANU WAKHLU, CO-AUTHOR

4

FROM LEGACY TO INNOVATION

BY

SHRAVAN GUPTA

"Look at the sky. We are not alone. The whole universe is friendly to us and conspires only to give the best to those who dream and work."

—APJ Abdul Kalam

In the summer of '98, I had just wrapped up my MBA at Vanderbilt University, Nashville. I was back in India with the sole intention of supporting my dad with his travel agency business. Founded back in '77, he had grown it into one of Bengaluru's most well-known travel agencies.

There was a time when I perceived my MBA as a ticket to a prestigious position with a substantial paycheck, perhaps within the banking sector or a sought-after consulting role.

But for me, it was more about my dad and my family. He put his heart into this business, and now he was facing a heap of financial and operational challenges. Moreover, he had been navigating through those challenges all alone. I figured that he could use a hand, and honestly, I could use a real-world challenge. I wanted to contribute and offer my support wherever possible, wherever I could make a difference for him.

I wasn't thinking too hard about the long game, so I just dove headfirst into the family business. It was a wild ride, to say the least.

Fast forward to 2003, I'm 29, knee-deep in the family business, recently married, and loving the new chapter of my life. And then, out of nowhere, my whole world is shaken up. My pillar, my father, is diagnosed with late-stage colorectal cancer. Before we could even grasp the situation, he passed away, leaving a massive void in the family and the business alike.

Enduring the loss of my father was an emotional upheaval like no other. The agony I experienced during this period made it challenging to process or feel much of anything. It was undoubtedly the greatest challenge I had faced so far, and yet, life didn't pause for my grief. My father was more than a boss; he was my North Star. His journey, starting as a pharmaceutical salesperson, with my mother by his side every step of the way, had been an arduous climb to establish and build our family business. Despite the challenges that came with a service background, they had toiled relentlessly throughout the years.

In the midst of grappling with the immense pain of losing my father, the relentless demands of life continued. Managing the family business and dealing with the complexities of tax and legal matters added an overwhelming layer of responsibility. The weight of these tasks felt even heavier against the backdrop of my deep personal grief. These tax cases and legal headaches were like uninvited guests barging in and making everything much more complicated. Boosting employee morale also became crucial at that point in time.

The usual rhythms of life persisted, and it was a struggle to navigate through each day. The business succession was nothing less than a chaotic circus, with its intricacies and uncertainties unfolding while I was still grappling with the void left by my father's absence.

Life's unyielding march forward, even in the face of my grief, presented an additional layer of difficulty.

In the midst of this emotional fog, I found myself traversing uncharted territory. The business challenges, coupled with the mourning process, demanded a resilience that felt beyond my reach at times. Yet, in the midst of the storm, I persevered, one step at a time, honoring not just the responsibilities at hand but also the memory of my father, whose guidance and strength had been an integral part of my life.

Encountering one life storm after another is quite the quirk of existence. Life, with its peculiar sense of humor, has never failed to surprise me.

The summer of 2005 marked a turning point in my life. In the wake of my father's passing in 2003 and the challenges that followed, those two years changed everything for me. As the dust settled on the tumultuous two years that had tested my resilience, I found myself standing at a crossroads, contemplating the path ahead.

The travel agency business, a legacy from my father, lay before me like a familiar but daunting terrain. Taking over my father's travel agency felt like standing at the edge of a known yet challenging territory. The industry was evolving, and the winds of change were blowing strong. The internet had become a game-changer, and I couldn't ignore the signs of consolidation and competition. Everything was changing in the travel industry, and the internet was at the heart of it. It wasn't just a tool; it was reshaping the entire game. Big players in travel were getting even bigger, and the landscape was shifting beneath our feet.

Ten years into the internet age in India, it wasn't just about information anymore. With the advent of cable internet in 2000, It was now where people planned and booked their journeys. Online platforms were making travel more accessible and changing what customers expected. The days of relying solely on physical offices were gone; now, success meant having a strong online presence.

This shift brought challenges. Big travel companies were using technology to streamline their operations and give customers better experiences. Online travel agencies (OTAs) were becoming popular, offering a place where customers could easily compare and book trips. It wasn't just a trend; it was a whole new way of doing things in the travel industry.

The tech-driven landscape prompted established travel companies to invest in adapting to new technologies, integrating them into operations with substantial investments and comprehensive training. Online platforms require businesses to establish a robust online presence through user-friendly websites and digital marketing to stay competitive. Evolving customer expectations compelled travel agencies to enhance customer service and provide seamless online booking experiences.

The rise of Online Travel Agencies (OTAs) posed a challenge, pushing traditional agencies to differentiate through unique services or a blend of online and offline offerings. Operational efficiency became critical, with larger companies leveraging technology and smaller businesses striving to keep pace.

As the industry burgeoned, data security and privacy concerns rose, making the safety of customer data a top priority. This led to investments in secure online platforms. In a saturated market, companies sought to differentiate through innovative strategies, be it unique travel packages, personalized services, or niche offerings, aiming to establish a distinctive identity.

Yet, amidst these challenges, the industry also grappled with the task of educating and engaging customers. Many were still tethered to traditional methods of travel planning, necessitating marketing strategies to enlighten and captivate them about the advantages and ease of using online platforms.

In that evolving landscape, navigating the challenges required not only adaptability but also an innovative and strategic approach to seamlessly incorporate technology while preserving customer satisfaction and trust. Adapting to that new digital world required a smart approach. It meant using digital marketing, or as it was known back then, internet marketing, to reach more people, making online booking systems efficient, and staying updated on the latest tech that could improve how customers experienced our services. Yet, amidst these challenges, the industry also grappled with the task of educating and engaging customers. Many were still tethered to traditional methods of travel planning, necessitating marketing strategies to enlighten and captivate them about the advantages and ease of using online platforms.

As an entrepreneur, this period demanded understanding the changes, predicting what might come next, and being flexible to adjust to the internet-driven market. The challenge was not just to survive but to thrive by using the internet to bring innovation and better service to the travel agency business.

Despite the comfort of familiarity, I couldn't shake the nagging question: Was continuing the travel agency business my true calling? Would it bring me the fulfillment, joy, and excitement that I sought in my professional life? It was time for introspection and a serious evaluation of my aspirations. The travel and tourism industry is a fascinating place and one that I had grown into thoroughly enjoying.

The allure of the internet beckoned. Its growing influence on the travel industry was undeniable, and I sensed an opportunity to carve out a niche in this evolving space. The challenges were different, but they were also exhilarating. The prospect of leveraging technology, exploring new avenues, and embracing innovation appealed to the entrepreneur in me.

Eventually, I took a bold step. Guided by a vision to embrace change and propel my family's legacy forward, I created the Travel Tours Group, a venture that would not only navigate the digital landscape but also redefine the way we approached travel. This would gradually grow into a group of eight distinct brands encompassing various sectors within the travel industry.

As I embarked on this entrepreneurial journey, the initial challenges were both invigorating and demanding. Building a robust online platform, staying ahead of technological advancements, and crafting a brand that resonated with the evolving consumer base required strategic thinking and swift execution.

The years that followed were a roller coaster of successes, setbacks, and lessons learned. The Travel Tours Group, under my stewardship, emerged as a prominent player in the travel space, offering innovative solutions and personalized experiences to our customers. The journey, however, was far from easy, with each milestone achieved through dedication, adaptability, and an unwavering commitment to excellence.

As the years unfolded, the travel industry became more than just a professional endeavor for me—it became a passion. The pulsating energy, the constant evolution, and the joy of creating memorable experiences for people fueled my determination to chart a unique course in this ever-expanding world.

Understanding the intricacies of the travel industry revealed to me its exciting facets. I wanted more than just a routine job; I aspired to create something extraordinary. Even as the Travel Tours Group was still a modest venture, I envisioned transforming it into a travel company that would capture the heart of the nation. I yearned to help people weave beautiful memories through our services. I have always believed that we have to have a purpose that goes beyond just transactions.

However, turning this vision into reality required more than just ambition. It demanded a formidable team that shared my passion and believed in the dream. The challenge was apparent—why would anyone choose a small business in Bengaluru over the allure of established hubs in Delhi and Mumbai? To overcome this hurdle, I found myself shuttling between these cities, tirelessly building connections, and selling my vision to potential team members.

The journey to assemble the right team was arduous, yet it laid the foundation for what would become an enviable and cohesive unit. A group of individuals who shared my enthusiasm and commitment to creating a travel company that stood out in a competitive landscape.

In a fortuitous turn of events, as I traversed this path, the Times of India group presented a unique opportunity. Their expansive media reach held the promise of visibility and growth for the Travel

Tours Group. In a groundbreaking initiative, they offered capital and media space in exchange for equity—an arrangement that seemed tailor-made for a business with grand aspirations but limited resources. The fact that a media giant like TOI considered us was a validation, a confidence boost that transcended the business transaction. It signaled that even a travel agency from Bengaluru had the potential to burgeon into something significant.

Emboldened by this partnership, Travel Tours Group stood at the precipice of a new era. The collaboration with the Times of India not only amplified our visibility but also bolstered our credibility in the industry. This was followed by a thrilling chapter that witnessed the metamorphosis of a modest travel agency into a national favorite, driven by passion, vision, and the unwavering belief that every journey holds the potential to create extraordinary memories.

The barter deal with the Times of India not only marked a significant milestone for Travel Tours Group but also opened doors to unparalleled growth. Our brands resonated across the country, gaining recognition and validation that instilled confidence in customers. The media presence became a testament to our reliability, and as the brand flourished, we set our sights on expanding our horizons.

For the next few years, our relentless focus was on organic growth, diversifying across verticals, geographies, and customer segments. In the ever-evolving landscape of online travel agents (OTA), we recognized the need to innovate. To complement our consumer-facing business, we ventured into the B2B space, becoming one of the largest wholesalers of non-air products in the country. Our reach extended to Sri Lanka, positioning us as the go-to partner for fulfilling diverse travel needs, from cruises to rail passes.

Recognizing the surge in incoming business to India and the rising demand for charters from Europe, we strategically acquired companies specializing in these sectors. An online specialist in domestic holiday packages also joined our portfolio of brands, reinforcing our position in the market. We became one of the few companies in the country to hold a category-II license from the Reserve Bank of India. Through this, we built an extensive network of foreign exchange units across the country.

By 2015, Travel Tours was not just a local player; we had expanded our footprint to 20 cities across India and Sri Lanka, boasting revenues exceeding USD 60 million. It was at this juncture that a message from a long-lost business associate set the stage for a new chapter in our journey.

The associate, now leading the India business for The Flight Centre Travel Group (FCTG), one of the largest travel companies globally, expressed a keen interest in our business. Negotiations, once initiated years ago, had not progressed, but circumstances had changed. FCTG saw numerous synergies with Travel Tours, offering an opportunity for mutual growth.

With Travel Tours poised for greater heights, I faced a crucial decision. The business was profitable and flourishing, but to compete on a global scale, we needed more resources. Aligning with FCTG through a cash and stock deal emerged as the solution, allowing us to access the necessary firepower for marketing and technology investments. The discussions even broached the prospect of an independent public listing in India.

The negotiation process was intense, fraught with challenges and moments of heartburn. Yet, both sides demonstrated maturity, navigating through complexities to finalize the deal in early 2017. At that point, our revenues had soared beyond USD 100 million, and the amalgamation with FCTG propelled the combined entity to the coveted rank of the second-largest travel business in India, according to the Times of India.

As the sun set on one chapter, the collaboration with FCTG heralded a new dawn for Travel Tours Group, promising a future of boundless possibilities in the global travel industry.

When an unexpected event suddenly looms on the horizon, especially one tied to a business nurtured for nearly two decades, emotions run high. This wasn't just a business; it was my father's legacy, a journey I'd been living and breathing for the past 18 to 19 years. The sudden realization that someone else saw immense value in it triggered a cascade of questions – were we missing something? Could we grow it ourselves? And what about the dedicated team that had stood by me over the years – how would they be treated? The uncertainty of what lay ahead cast a shadow over the familiar landscape I had grown so attached to. The decision also bore the essence of a family choice, and I consider myself fortunate to have received wholehearted support from my family throughout this journey.

The subsequent two years became an emotional roller coaster. The pivotal question hung in the air – sell or not? If the decision leaned towards selling, the path forked into considerations of a full sale versus earning out, the composition of cash and stock, and the intricate dance of valuation. The weight of these decisions was immense, requiring careful contemplation of the future and the legacy that had been painstakingly built.

Once the dust settled and a deal was agreed upon, a new phase commenced – a phase laden with the challenges of due diligence. However, perhaps the most demanding task lay in front – communicating this transformative decision to the team. The emotional aspect of the journey became palpable as I navigated the delicate task of helping my dedicated team comprehend the rationale behind this strategic move.

The road to finalizing the deal was fraught with conditions precedent – a stressful period of announcing the deal, managing warranties, navigating novation, overseeing employee transfers, and ensuring seamless client communication. The intricacies of the business transaction demanded a fastidious approach to ensure a smooth transition from one phase to the next.

In February 2017, as the deal concluded, the combined entity emerged as the second-largest in India, boasting a turnover of USD 400 million. The validation of this transformative acquisition was underscored by the fact that on the very day, the deal was announced, the Flight Centre share price soared by 6%, a testament to the strategic prowess and success of the acquisition. The journey,

from emotional upheaval to strategic decision-making and deal
conclusion, was a multifaceted exploration of the complexities
inherent in transitioning a business from one set of hands to another.

The integration of the two businesses loomed as the next
significant challenge – a complex puzzle involving people, processes,
and software. It was a scrupulous process that required not just
aligning operations but merging cultures and visions. Tough
decisions had to be made, and they came with a heavy emotional toll.
The most poignant of these decisions involved parting ways with
individuals who had weathered the storm with us through thick and
thin. Letting go of loyal team members was undoubtedly the most
heart-wrenching aspect of the post-acquisition phase.

Despite the difficulties, I remained on the board for two years.
This period proved to be a phenomenal experience, working
collaboratively with bright minds from across the globe. The synergy
of diverse perspectives and expertise was invaluable. Together, we
embarked on a journey of scaling the business to new heights,
crossing the impressive milestone of USD 550 million in that time
frame.

The process of integration was not just about merging financials
and operations; it was about weaving together the unique threads of
each entity into a cohesive tapestry. Every decision carried the
weight of its impact on the people who had been an integral part of
the journey. It was a period of challenges, growth, and evolution, a
time when the resilience of the team and the adaptability of the
business strategies came to the forefront.

As I reflect on those two years, I can't help but appreciate the
learnings, the relationships forged, and the collective effort that went
into not just sustaining but elevating the business. The journey didn't
end with the acquisition; it evolved into a chapter marked by
collaboration, innovation, and the relentless pursuit of excellence.
Let me walk you through the intricacies of steering a business
through the nuances of integration and growth in the dynamic
landscape of the global market. Reflecting on the process of closing
this deal, several key insights emerged:

1. **Aligned Leadership is Crucial:** The success of a deal hinges on aligned leadership. It is essential that all parties involved share a common vision and actively desire the deal's success. Despite the inevitable challenges that may arise, it is crucial to maintain focus on the initial motivations that sparked the deal.

2. **Balancing Give and Take:** Negotiations involve a delicate balance of give and take. Objectivity is paramount; carefully selecting non-negotiables ensures a balanced agreement that serves the interests of both parties. Striking this balance is instrumental in fostering a healthy and mutually beneficial collaboration.

3. **Expert Advisors are Indispensable:** Within the intricacies of deals, having the right financial and legal advisors is non-negotiable. Their expertise serves as a guiding compass, navigating the complexities of negotiations and ensuring that all aspects are thoroughly vetted and understood.

4. **Transparency with the Team is Key:** The team plays a pivotal role during the transition phase, and transparency is the cornerstone of effective leadership. Open communication about the changes, challenges, and the rationale behind the deal is essential. This transparency not only fosters trust but also helps alleviate the stress that accompanies a period of transition.

5. **Active Involvement in Due Diligence:** Due diligence is not a passive process; it demands active engagement. Being fully involved in scrutinizing every aspect of the deal ensures a comprehensive understanding, mitigating potential risks and paving the way for a smoother transition.

6. **Navigating Challenges with a Trusted Team:** Challenges are inevitable, and conditions precedent can be particularly demanding. Having a trusted group of individuals around you, capable of navigating challenges and getting things done, is invaluable. This support system becomes the backbone during the intricate phases of a deal.

These learnings encapsulate the essence of successfully navigating the complexities inherent in closing a deal, serving as a roadmap for future endeavors in the dynamic landscape of business negotiations.

Post the acquisition and transition, I decided to take a sabbatical from all operating businesses. During this time, I set up our family office and used the time to spend with my family and enjoy my hobbies. Despite the relaxation and the slow pace of my life, the entrepreneur in me remained unsatisfied. Energy levels dipped as a sense of incompleteness loomed. Then, at this critical juncture, a friend presented a unique idea—fractional ownership of luxury second homes.

As I delved into the concept, my conviction grew. It wasn't just a business idea; it was a venture that resonated with me quite profoundly, also striking my curiosity. The prospect of fractional ownership in luxury properties sparked excitement and ignited the dormant entrepreneurial spirit within.

Starting or scaling a business requires a meticulous focus on critical factors. The five pillars for business success, as I see them, are:

- **The Idea:** A revolutionary concept that challenges the status quo and addresses a genuine need.
- **The Team:** A cohesive and capable team, each member contributing unique skills and perspectives.
- **The Funding:** Adequate financial support to fuel growth and innovation.
- **The Business Model - Revenue and Costs:** A sustainable and scalable model ensuring a balance between scale and profitability.
- **The Timing:** Recognizing and seizing the opportune moment to launch or expand.

The genesis of this venture was rooted in the aspiration to create a new category—one that navigates the intricacies of awareness, regulations, and structure. Embarking on this journey, self-funded and exploring uncharted territory, is undeniably challenging yet remarkably thrilling. Merging the realms of property, technology, and real estate, the venture, aptly named YOURS, is set to revolutionize how people perceive, use, and manage their second homes.

As the gears of this new venture begin to turn, the anticipation is palpable. The challenges are inherent, but the prospect of carving a niche in an unexplored domain adds an exhilarating dimension to my entrepreneurial journey. The narrative unfolds, and the story of YOURS takes its place in the ever-evolving tapestry of innovation and business exploration.

AUTHOR BIO

Shravan built and ran the Travel Tours Group, a major player in the Indian tourism sector, and he has been involved with the tourism and hospitality industry for over 25 years. He acquired a Bachelors of Commerce degree from Bangalore University and an MBA from Vanderbilt University.

He accelerated the growth of Travel Tours Group into one of India's leading travel businesses with operations across 20 cities in India and Sri Lanka. The group included brands like Travel Air Representations, Travel Air, Splendour Holidays, Go Avenues, Mustseeindia.com and Migradocs Immigration Services. The business ranged from providing retail travel services to being an authorized money changer with a Cat 2 license from the RBI, and had a specialized inbound division that handled charters into Goa. The Rs. 800 crore Travel Tours Group was later acquired by Flight Centre Australia in early 2017, and the combined business was ranked as the second-largest travel enterprise in India by the Times of India.

Shravan then set up Kriya Ventures, a family office with interests in education, travel tech, hospitality, children's fitness and real estate. He founded the Tattva School and Sports Academy, which is now one of the leading CBSE schools in Bangalore with over 700 children.

He has been the Past President of the Entrepreneurs Organisation (EO) Bangalore chapter and a regional council member of the EO South Asia region. He has served as the Chairman of the Tourism Committee of Bangalore Chamber of

Industry and Commerce (BCIC) and has been on the board of Mumbai Angels. He serves on the Board of Trustees of various education and social non-profit organizations like Vasavi Trust, Karnataka Arya Vysya Charitable Trust and RANG Foundation. RANG Foundation supports talented children who wish to pursue a career in sports.

Some of his past and current startup investments include Ixigo.com, Goodera, The Little Gyms of India, Pathfindr.io. He has been featured on CNBC Young Turks and is a regular speaker/panelist at various industry events.

He loves to golf and is also a hobby actor. He has played the lead in an independent film called 'Daemon' that is available on Amazon Prime globally and on YouTube in India.

Shravan, along with his co-founders, is now building YOURS - a business offering fractional ownership of luxury second homes. This unique concept is a first in India and aims to change the way people buy, own and use luxury second homes.

SHRAVAN GUPTA, CO-AUTHOR

5

CONQUERING THE UNKNOWN – THE INSPIRATIONAL TALE OF ENTREPRENEURIAL TRIUMPH

BY

DEEPAK MOHLA

"Discovering who you are today is the first step to being who you will be

tomorrow."

–Anonymous

In a world filled with constant noise and distractions, the journey of self-discovery emerges as a quiet oasis amidst the chaos. It transcends the realm of superficial assessments and dives deep into the recesses of our souls, unearthing the essence of our being. While discovering who you are and how you want to live your life, it is vital to understand your life's purpose. To me, defining and giving yourself to a clear and larger purpose in life will motivate you to thrive better at opportunities. In the voyage of figuring out your purpose in life, you will encounter various landmarks and milestones that contribute to your self-awareness.

These may include moments of vulnerability, where you confront your fears and insecurities head-on, emerging more robust and more resilient. These encounters become catalysts for growth, helping you shed old layers of conditioning and stepping into the fullness of your potential. I have had my fair share of struggles, too, but after aligning myself with my purpose to make my life count, everything fell into place.

To begin with, I was born in a middle-class family in Delhi to parents who had moved to the city just before the violence of the Partition had left its indelible mark on thousands of people caught in that vortex. My father greatly respected education since he was an officer in the Education Ministry Central Govt. He ensured that all his five children were given the best opportunities in Education despite the modest means at his disposal. Therefore, I spent the first eight years of schooling at St. Columba's and the last three years at the Modern High School.

Since I was exceptional in Chemistry, I joined Hansraj College, Delhi University, with Chemistry Honors. The three years mainly were spent not in the lecture rooms but in different parts of the campus with friends, having coffee at India Coffee House, or snacking at the many places Delhi University had to offer students newfound independence.

After graduation, I completed my MBA from FMS Delhi and was offered the opportunity to work at Rallis, a part of the Tata Group, in Mumbai. Over the next 25 years, I traversed my journey from a Management Trainee to various roles in Sales & Marketing in different companies— Rallis, Escorts & Modi Xerox. Subsequently, I moved into SBU Head roles in Modi Xerox & later in Escorts.

My last assignment was with a large Indian group as the Managing Director of the holding company. In brief, that was the first part of my professional career— a corporate avatar. The second part of my journey has been and continues to be as an Entrepreneur in the Management Consulting domain— Leadership & Organization

Development. Therefore, my professional life of over fifty years is split equally between the Corporate and the Entrepreneurial.

When I began working in my first organization, my boss had the idea of giving me a small task and letting me experiment and learn from it. He gave me the freedom to have my own approach to fulfilling any task. However, when he found that the operation had become much more extensive than he had anticipated, he wanted to have some control. To be honest, I do not respond very positively to control. Fortunately, I have had bosses who probably saw something in me and encouraged me to explore & experiment. They gave me the space when it was possible, but I had problems and conflicts wherever the space was unavailable. Since I often realized that I like to have my own space and work innovatively, I wanted to build something for myself and call it my own. Even while doing my regular job, somewhere deep down, I felt I was fit for entrepreneurship.

My independent attitude and innovative approach have become a strength of mine. I left a massive role as the Head of Sales for Business & joined Modi Xerox to start something totally fresh, which meant there was only me to begin with. Initially, I was frustrated thinking about what I was supposed to do as there was no clear & big vision for the business opportunity I was entrusted with. It was a small business, and I struggled a lot in the first three months. I remember my Director telling me that the number of complaints from some stakeholders would have put this business on the *critical* map in the Xerox world!

I was quite taken aback by that because I was seeing myself as a reasonably good performer. Albeit shocked, I assured him I would create a process to ensure the problems get sorted. I led a team of five people and began a process that would ensure that the stakeholders' requirements were always fully met. The new process was recognized and awarded as one of the best projects in the entire Xerox world. Since then, the journey towards self-growth began. For me, creating processes to improve performance and solving chronic issues became a way of thinking and building greenfield business units — small or large. Sustainability comes through processes, and institution-building requires processes. I believe in institutions, so process thinking and building processes have become a critical part of my personality.

Today, when I look back, I see that I had a reasonably successful corporate career. Starting as a management trainee, I traversed the journey to becoming the managing director of a multi-business group, **Modicorp** (BK MODI GROUP), and achieved many firsts on the way. Perhaps my innate desire to put conventional wisdom aside and try to experiment to enjoy the journey contributed to my success. As a very young man, for my first posting, I was given a small job with some degree of independence since it was in a remote location. My boss thought I might not do too much damage but maybe learn. But to their surprise, in the eighteen months I was there, I transformed the new sales office into the country's most prominent sales office. I did not realize that I had achieved something significant; I felt that maybe it had just happened. I was transferred to the head office and given a new job that did not exist earlier— a Product Manager. I asked myself what I should be doing as there was no precedent to follow. I recall an incident from that time which I would like to share with you, dear reader.

I was sitting in a meeting to finalize the budget for next year with the Regional Heads and the Director of the Business, along with my supervisor and other departmental Heads. The Regional Managers wanted a lower target, and the Director was keen to have substantially higher targets because he felt the opportunity was good. There was no fundamental rationale or data to support either of the arguments, and eventually, a middle ground was agreed upon.

I should bring some logic into the process of business plans for next year. Over the next six months, I traveled across the country, read many research reports, etc. & created a 5-year strategic plan for the business.

Looking back at it, it was a significant turning point in my career. We were operating at that time at around 40% capacity utilization. My plan suggested that in five years, we would need three times the capacity that we have today. As I had expected, the plan met with much resistance, but the logic was irrefutable. Hence, they accepted a toned-down business target, which yielded a much higher performance. I found myself struggling with anything conventional and repetitive. I found it to be very dull and felt I might fail. To make the job enjoyable, I would create my challenges by creating new processes and setting higher or different goals. Today, when I look back at the past, I realize that change is necessary for me.

During my second stint with Escorts Kubota, when I was the business head for the tractors business, I faced a disruptive situation. There was a family business for which I had given my guarantee against the loans taken for plant & machinery. However, the business ran into significant financial stress. Due to this situation, the business was not flourishing, and the banks were sending notices. I had no option but to leave my job, take over the family business, and try to turn it around. However, there was no money that I could draw from this business. Ironically, the company was consuming cash and not generating any. I started a small consulting company to create some cashflow. At that time, I had two businesses running simultaneously -one was the manufacturing unit for automotive components and the other was the consulting business where I focused on helping small businesses develop their business strategy for growth.

Within 18 months after turning around the auto component business, I returned it to the family member running it while I continued with my consulting. My last consulting assignment was with Dr. B.K Modi, who was known for the number of joint venture companies he had at that time. He knew me because of my stint at Xerox Joint Venture. Dr. Modi wanted to bring all individual businesses together in a holding company and create an organization to manage the growth of the Group. I worked with him as a consultant for 6-8 months and helped him make the holding company. After that, I joined him as a Chief Strategy Officer. That was a solid learning period for me because I had opportunities to work globally with some of the best names in the world— Telstra

Australia for telecom, with Xerox, and with Alcatel for Telecom equipment.

During those six years, I traveled around the world supporting Dr. Modi in managing the holding company and the many joint Ventures. At that time, the holding company concept was at a very nascent stage, and most of the large groups were content to let the Operating companies run independently with virtually no writ in the management of these companies. For financing of new projects, the holding company needed to organize funds.

We engaged global consultants, but they believed that no one would invest at the holding company level. The CFO and Dr. Modi tried but failed to get investors. I offered to help and try to raise investment resources.

One of the major celebrations of my career was when I managed to raise equity from a Singapore-based company. The Government of Singapore has many investing arms. I got that investment and proved global consultants wrong that even in a holding company, you could get equity. This particular incident built a lot of confidence in me, and I decided that I could give entrepreneurship a chance. I learned a lot working with Dr. Modi because the canvas to operate on was very big, and I had the liberty to explore.

I had observed that, over the six years I had worked with the holding company, dealing with the CEOs and the senior management team, I had a natural affinity to connect with them. There was a feeling of trust I could get with them, and then help resolve mutual issues and even partner level conflicts. During that period, I joined a couple of BODs of startups as an independent director. I observed that the young entrepreneurs required a lot of hand-holding and needed someone to talk to who they could trust. That was when I started mentoring those entrepreneurs more about business strategy, organization, and leadership development. Around the same time, an opportunity arose for me to take the partnership of Time Manager International (TMI) for India.

In all honesty, the beginning of my entrepreneurial journey came to me by accident. There was no specific moment when I committed myself entirely to this journey. The transition happened smoothly when I realized I wanted to make an impact in two ways— a) run a business; b) be a leadership coach/mentor. We invited a Management Guru, Claus Moeller, to India to run some seminars. Claus was one of the nine Quality gurus of the world and one who focused on the human side of quality. He had a great style of delivery. When I saw him keeping 200 people firmly committed to their seats for one whole day, I realized the power he wielded through his oratory skills. He had people mesmerized listening to each word of us. Seeing him, I realized that I, too, wanted to be able to hold people spellbound for a full day without getting up.

Everyone faces a lot of challenges in their lives. Whenever I face any challenge, I do not feel a sense of discontinuity/disruption. The challenges tend to infuse energy as they force you to solve/manage them – all this takes thinking and action. Having a strong leaning toward being creative would result in some unusual approaches being taken – not always successful! I think I was already in an entrepreneurial mode in my few years with Dr. Modi because I could understand his thinking process and be aligned with the same quite often. Moreover, I realized that I was pretty content to take risks and live with ambiguity despite a very strong need for seeking information in making decisions. I think getting into an entrepreneurial groove was simple as I was also a process thinker. An entrepreneur is not necessarily a very process-driven person, but a professional is. In our consulting business we have all the processes, which a large company could be proud of.

Therefore, when I say entrepreneurial, it means doing something new— it was always something where there was no one to tell me what to do. I wanted to set goals and have a sense of freedom. My entrepreneurial journey happened very organically. I will give destiny some credit as well. One thing I recommend that everybody should keep in mind is to work to their strengths. This is something I learned from a client who is now the Managing Director of a large Private Bank. Back then, he made the assertion, " I want people to focus on their strengths, and not on their weaknesses. They are not going to create value for the Organization by focusing on their weaknesses." I thought that was a very profound statement because weaknesses will not become your strengths. You can mitigate them so they do not stop you from using your strengths. If you make your strengths work for you, then that is where you are going to create value for yourself and others. In retrospect, I realize I was probably utilizing my strengths. Hence, I would not have enjoyed it if I had to do something with operations or similar repetitive roles.

When you are very independent, there is also a downside, low collaboration. I started discovering myself as a leader as I was helping others to find themselves. Things that I got to know about myself helped me in my transition to being an entrepreneur as I started leveraging my strengths. I think the business could have grown much bigger if that were to be my motivator or purpose. You might think I was preceding the opportunities to grow big, but that was not my aspiration. I never wanted to create a large organization. I wanted to create a good organization, a good legacy, and develop people internally. As far as I am concerned, I believe I did good for myself.

When I began this journey, I had a few doubts, but I was fortunate that my wife was also a partner. There was a degree of trust and comfort, which only some have. Collaboration or partnership, which is a challenge for husband and wife, is not a great combination for running a business. But be that as it may, there was a degree of dependence and availability of good counsel all the time. I think those were when the question— "You want to grow, but should you want to grow that? How would you grow?" arose.

We enjoyed doing what we did and developed the organization over the years. Our approach is always to develop our employees. We were not focused on how to make a lot of money. We hired from some of the best institutes of psychology and trained them. Over the years, hundreds of people have worked with us & learned from us, which has been a very fulfilling part.

During my journey, I had the fortune of meeting a few people who inspired me with their own experiences and their impact on others. When I was the Managing Director of the holding company,

Mr. K.L.Chugh, who was the former chairman of ITC became my guide and counselor. He would encourage me to think big and seize opportunities wisely. As a person who believes in developing people and building the Organization, I think one of the best pieces of advice he gave us was— Create on your own. If you are in this business, you cannot copy someone else's work. "Do what you must to create your own? What is core for you?" he would say. "Think big. Be independent" and never rely on anyone else. I think that was very important and helped us a lot. It helped us set up a whole development ecosystem and build our identity, culture, and organization.

Based on our research, we developed & created our leadership development programs. We came up with white papers and research papers, especially on areas like emotional intelligence, leadership development, and customer-centric cultures. We started our consulting business under the banner of TMI Associates in partnership with TMI Global. We changed our name to **INSPIREONE** after six years because we wanted to own our identity, our destiny and not be limited to what our partners do globally. We entered into more partnerships and always focused on what value we bring to the customers we serve.

The whole idea of ensuring that people stay in your company for a long time is very challenging for any entrepreneur. Especially for a small company, it is always going to be a challenge, irrespective of whichever industry you are with. Some people can stay with you for ten to twelve years. For some, it is even less. Of course, a couple of them stayed with us for a very long time. Attrition is a problem that any kind of business, whether large, small, medium, or even corporates, faces.

Technology is always going to play a big part in the business that we are in. We started using technology before COVID-19, and this helped the company tide through the trying times of the pandemic! In our business, the Brandon Hall Award is considered the industry's Oscar. In the last three years, we have won one award each year because we use blended learning, technology, simulations, etc., and are very focused on helping our clients solve business issues by helping people build better capabilities.

The time during COVID-19 was challenging as the business that we are in always had a face-to-face interaction. We were conducting workshops and coaching people. Most of the organizations during this time collapsed, but we were able to navigate this better since we had already harnessed technology to create solutions. We were the first to partner with IBM Watson to use AI for leadership assessments. During the lockdown period, we read, made calls over Zoom, and even conducted workshops over Zoom. We were able to adapt very quickly, and we were lucky due to our forward thinking. The core technology helped us to navigate this period. It was tough, but we managed.

Managing costs, keeping the morale high, and returning to work from the office took us about two years. The lockdown period was when we had to motivate the team and be eager to try new things. It was pretty tough, both financially and mentally. Since my default thought process is more like a professional rather than an entrepreneur, I could survive the difficult times. There are moments when I wonder how people will identify me. They will probably see me as the owner. I dislike the word owner because it gives you a sense of aloofness from the rest of the team. Therefore, I do not use that term because I do not want people to see me in that light.

Before my entrepreneurial journey, I focused on large business-related strategic issues. My strengths have always revolved around-- thinking big, strategy, greenfield, etc. Today, when I look back at it, my thinking has shifted from business strategy to a more focused people & institution thinking. This transition happened more toward the end of my corporate career. This journey has changed me in so many ways. My way of understanding people has improved enormously, including my self-awareness. I can understand people better; I can understand why they react a certain way. I believe I can help them to improve their professional & social capability. This has been an enormous sense of comfort to me. I bring value by helping people understand and be comfortable with themselves.

I was very fortunate to have a couple of business partners who could think like me and who were there for the love of it. I believe that enjoying what you do is far better than doing it only for money. Hence, I like coming to the office, sharing ideas, and meeting my team, my clients. There has always been some degree of enjoyment and passion in it. Contributing and giving it a more significant purpose is very important for me. We sincerely help people become better than what they were before they met with us. Therefore, we can build their potential and unlock it for them. If I had to start this journey now, I would begin it earlier this time. One thing is that you need to be physically in your prime. There are better times to start an enterprise than the age of fifty. Therefore, I would not begin at fifty; I would have probably started eight to ten years earlier. If anyone starts afresh as an entrepreneur, it is better to begin with a few like-minded people. It helps as, though independence is good, interdependence is better. Therefore, I would do that differently.

If I had to offer advice to a budding entrepreneur, knowing your strengths and playing to your strengths is the number one thing. The second important thing is to create a support system. The third thing is to be independent and yet collaborate with others.

At this phase of my work life, I have realized that I play two roles— A professional leader in an organization and an institution builder. I want to segregate the two because I do not want the organization to close just because I am retiring. I want it to live. It is the biggest challenge that I am grappling with now. Even after moving out, I want to play a small role and continue mentoring.

The moment individuals find the courage to believe in their unique light, they unlock a limitless potential. Once you build confidence in yourself, following the crowd seems redundant. The voyage of life is only sometimes smooth sailing.

At times, I was caught in the tempestuous seas of adversity, the furious waves threatening to capsize my dreams. But even in the midst of such turbulence, my confidence and purpose of life stood resolute. Everyone has a different journey: I had mine, too, and this was how I did it. I hope you figure out your purpose, too, and align yourself with it. So, are you ready to embark on your extraordinary journey of self-discovery, resilience, and transformation? I pray you unlock the keys to your true potential, unravel the mysteries of success, and traverse uncharted territories of growth.

AUTHOR BIO

Deepak Mohla, Chairman & Managing Director of Inspireone Consultants & Chairman of Inspireone Technologies, boasts nearly fifty years of diverse experience spanning corporate roles, consulting, leadership development, and coaching. An MBA graduate from the Faculty of Management Studies, Delhi, and a Chemistry (Hons) graduate from the University of Delhi, he exhibits a steadfast commitment to innovation and experimentation. Beginning his career at Rallis India, a Tata Group company, Deepak subsequently held pivotal leadership positions at Escorts and Modi Xerox, leaving indelible marks through pioneering strategies. His tenure with Modicorp, supporting Dr. B.K. Modi, culminated in the establishment of a strategic-level holding company. Transitioning to human resources, Deepak founded Inspireone Consultants, focusing on People and Organisation Development. Partnering with TACK TMI, the company has impacted over 400 organizations and 200,000 individuals, counting Tata Motors, Unilever, and Airtel among its clients. Deepak personally specializes in Senior Leadership Development and Organisation Change, earning recognition as a coach, consultant, and innovator. He and his wife Neeta are proud parents of two sons, two daughters-in-law, and three grandchildren.

DEEPAK MOHLA, CO-AUTHOR

6

FROM MUMBAI SLUMS TO BSE TRIUMPH: A JOURNEY OF DREAMS

BY

DR. MOHAMMED ASLAM KHAN

"If your dreams don't scare you, they are too small."

– Richard Branson

As the sun sets on a bustling city, painting the sky in hues of orange and magenta, my father, the visionary, the backbone, the driving fuel behind everything that I am today, stands on a rooftop, a silhouette against the backdrop of towering buildings. Throughout his life, he shielded me and my siblings no matter how much he had to toil for us. He was the guiding force who sculpted me and my siblings, ingraining in us values of independence, resilience, and self-reliance. We grew up in the Mumbai airport slum, consisting of nine family members living in a 9 ft x 9ft hut. As you can already understand, I did not have a fancy childhood and had been in the face of adversity innumerable times.

When you embark on a voyage to an uncharted territory, you often get equipped with a compass of self-reflection and a map of personal growth. With each step forward, you encounter unexplored facets of your identity, casting aside the veil of ignorance and embracing the rich tapestry of your life. As I moved ahead with each phase of my journey, I recounted all the teachings imparted to me by my father and how much he wanted me to break away the shackles of poverty and emerge victorious.

My father was a bread seller in Mumbai. He used to collect bread and sell them in the Southern Mumbai high rise towers consisting of 20 to 40 floors. During that time, hawkers were not allowed to use lift or escalators. One fine day, after he delivered the bread on the respective floor, he felt very thirsty. Since he did not know English, he could not communicate with anyone and he had to use signals to convey his thirst. Unfortunately, people misinterpreted him thinking he was asking for alcohol early in the morning. When they realized that he actually wanted water, the whole room burst into laughter and my father was deeply embarrassed by the situation. It was the first time in life he understood the importance of education. Since then, my father vowed to himself that no matter what happens in life, he will make sure that his children never have to be in an embarrassing situation like this.

Despite the circumstances that we grew up in, my father made sure that all of us receive proper education and stand on our own feet someday. He never wanted us to go through the hardships that he had to endure all his life. He enrolled me in the Bombay Municipal Corporation, which was a government free schooling. Ever since I was a child, I dreamt of doing something big in life. I never wanted my circumstances to define me and serve as a hindrance from aiming high. There is a saying that "if you can imagine it, you can achieve it; if you can dream it, you can become it." Today, I finally feel my dream has come true. The journey from being Aslam Khan and studying in a government school to getting my engineering degree from the Mumbai University, to doing Ph.D. in Business Management and Postdoctoral Research Fellowship in

Social entrepreneurship from the Markfield Institute, Leicester, UK, and acquiring the title of Dr. Mohammed Aslam Khan, I have come a long way. And needless to say, this journey would not have been possible without my beloved father.

When my father was selling bread, he wanted to get a better job and support his family even more. In front of the Bombay Stock Exchange, there is an Indian Navy office. After toiling hard for so many years in his life, my father wanted to take the job of a gatekeeper because he liked the idea of wearing a uniform. From having the minimal choice of changing into a better job to watching his son being listed at the Bombay Stock Exchange in the year 2017, it was a huge moment of pride for him.

So, are you wondering when did the enthusiasm for business spark within me? Well, my father told me in my childhood that having a business will bring me more financial freedom than a regular job. Since then, I have had a zeal for building a company from scratch and running the business on my own. As I grew up, I had the belief that the best way to create a positive impact in society, both at the economic and social level is through entrepreneurship. As mentioned, this was encouraged by my father's constant motivation to start a business. Though he could not make enough in his scrap trading business, he provided shelter and support to migrant workers from Uttar Pradesh in his scrap shop. The spiritual belief that "9 out of 10 of sustenance are from business" encourages individuals to venture into business. Therefore, this path drew me to my vision towards entrepreneurship.

Every big dream has to start from somewhere. I began mine while starting my career as a Software Analyst in 1996 with Tata Consultancy Services. Later on, I moved to Tokyo, Japan to work for Citibank till 1998. After that, I relocated to Seattle, USA in 1998 to work for Microsoft Corporation, Redmond, USA. Over there, I joined Dotcom and continued working in Seattle, USA as the Director of Engineering and headed the India Software delivery Centre with a salary in USD six figures till 2006. I spent my days working, reading books, learning, enhancing my horizons of knowledge, and helping freshers with internships and jobs by sharing technical knowledge to get the job in the industry.

Before I started my business, there was a specific moment that sparked the beginning of my entrepreneurial journey. During the year 2002-2003 in Seattle, I was assigned the responsibility of offshore development of building the enterprise software product. I experienced that outsourcing from the USA to India for software programming with regards to cost saving (cheap labor) was easy in terms of finding a software coder, but for product development, there was a lack of "software solution architect", as there was no startup culture in India that time – an opportunity which required the services in a niche area. Therefore, I wanted to come back to India and build my own startup company to serve this unmet market need.

With regards to coming back to India, I had two things in mind. The first thing was that my parents were growing old, so they would need attention and care. In fact, my father was the first person to oppose my decision when I informed him about returning to India. His reason was that when his son is in the USA, there is a lot of respect and pride for him in the neighborhood. After all, being in the United States used to be a matter of social respect during that time. However, my parents did not want to migrate to the US after staying for sixty years in India. For this reason, I had a fear lurking behind me. When my father migrated from Uttar Pradesh to Mumbai, his intention was to provide a good education and a better life for his children. Due to this struggle, he could never go back to his parents and when he lost them, he could not join the last rituals. I did not want to repeat this history and have regrets throughout my life.

The second thing that bothered me was— I would contemplate for a long time whether there is a significant contribution I am making in the economic development of the nation that made me where I am. The nation that contributes to shaping our lives by providing free education— how much do we contribute/give back to the nation once we become successful? By living the American life, we can contribute financially, but it is difficult to serve and contribute remotely. Truth to be told— when people travel to the US, they garner a green card citizenship, and lose the will to come back to India.

If all talented people from India migrate and settle abroad, then the economic development of that country will increase and our own country will lose its prospects. If this process continues, how will India grow as a country? That was when I contemplated— India is where my roots belong and my country has given me the education and resources that I needed to be a Developer in Microsoft Windows operating system. Therefore, how can I help my country to be a nation supplying/offering operating systems to the world? I wanted to make a change and do something magnanimous in my own country. This has been my thought process and I would be delighted to see more entrepreneurs from India carving their mark within the country.

I also wondered that once my child starts going to school in the USA, it would become all the more complicated to relocate to India. After a lot of retrospection, we decided to shift to India terminating the USA green card with a single focus in mind— to start the entrepreneurial journey in India serving the USA market in order to solve the pain area of the product architecture gap. I had a strong conviction of fulfilling my dream no matter what obstacle came by. The entrepreneurial journey of building **"Octaware Technologies Limited"** – An IT solution and services firm) from scratch began after ten years of job experience in the industry.

The business plan was drafted, reviewed, and vetted before taking the leap. Therefore, I had no resistance or hesitation.

Finally, in September 2006, I left the American dream of living in the United States and came back to India. I thought of fulfilling my childhood dream of building my own business. Therefore, I started the entrepreneurial journey with a monthly salary of 10% of the last drawn executive salary. I began working around sixteen to eighteen hours per day throughout the week. I had to get on to late night calls for the business development with the USA client, and at daytime building delivery and operations team. It was very hectic and tiresome but I never gave up. It was the moment when I fully committed myself to this journey. In 2008, after the financial crisis in the USA market, I started traveling to pivot the business model to focus on the MENA region.

Like any other start-up, there were a few challenges initially. During the conceptual stage of building the startup, I had built a team with talented professionals, but they had high ambitions and did not kick start. Thus, I had to focus on building the team with trustworthy professionals. I onboarded those trustworthy professionals by offering co-founder equity and executive leadership roles in the company. Acquiring the first few customers was a little difficult but with time, things became better. I personally focused on business development through the "sales partner" network. I got involved in ensuring quality delivery to the customers and after-delivery support, and adopted the model of equity-based delivery to acquire the first few customers. There was also the challenge of attracting and retaining talent. The development of a purposeful vision and mission of the organization was important. We developed our vision to serve, add value, and create growth for individuals, businesses, and social entities. The deputation of employees to the USA was necessary to retain employees even though there was a loss in the business deal. We also began developing a learning culture at the organization by offering an MBA to people who wanted to learn.

As I moved ahead towards my goal, the challenges intensified. There was a tough time faced during the listing of Octaware Technologies at the Bombay Stock Exchange (BSE), India. The fundraising was planned by inviting NRIs and foreigners from the USA and MENA to invest in the first fully Shariah-compliant company receiving the nod from BSE, mostly NRIs and Foreigners leveraging the newly launched FPI (Foreign Portfolio Investor) scheme. However, this scheme failed due to the complications of documentation and the cost involved. It seemed like the IPO would fail, but a solution of FDI (Foreign Direct Investment) with an intermediary investment vehicle incorporating the delegated authority structure was implemented as a way of problem-solving. The most critical challenge during the journey was acquiring the EOU (Export Oriented Unit) office in SEEPZ-SEZ (Special Economic Zone) in 2015.

Even after making 100% payment, it took around eighteen months to take over the possession to shift the business to the new office. It was a conflict with the ethical approach— aligning with the ecosystem/culture. We appointed a liaisoning team to address all regulatory queries, building local administrative relationships, and leveraging the state and central government support at a higher level helped resolve the issues.

After overcoming that significant challenge, there was a moment of reprieve when the SEEPZ-SEZ office was right in front of the company from where the career started twenty years back for the co-founders. It helped in the business growth by attracting the right talent. It was also an exciting moment when this case study was picked up by Prof Saumitra Jha of Stanford Graduate School of Business at the "Business Ethics" session of the SEED leadership program at Stanford GSB. Also, one of the purposes was to comply with the Shariah-compliant method of the company's valuation— a 10% of the company's value should be composed of physical assets.

One of the biggest achievements in my life was to get the company listed on the Bombay Stock Exchange within ten years of the formation of the company. The first presentation made to the employees in 2006 mentioned a 10-year roadmap with IPO, and it was achieved by filing the draft prospectus in 2016. The final listing with a successful IPO happened in 2017. The second company **"Transpact"**, a therapeutic medical devices company, also got listed in 2019 at BSE-Startup— the first startup to list on the startup platform of BSE. After achieving the above-mentioned goals, I launched a business incubator, **"GoBizLab"** – A Centre for Innovation and Entrepreneurship Development Center to help youth and budding entrepreneurs in their business model and entrepreneurship development. The plan was to write books to share the experience and knowledge gained with the success of the businesses and failures— three ventures started that had to be shut down.

During my journey, I had a few allies who supported me along the way. The successful model of equity-based partnership with the co-founding team worked. While developing and growing the IT company; Octaware, other businesses in healthcare were also built in 2008 on a similar model of equity-sharing in the business partnership— **(Multi-speciality Hospital/Diagnostic center - Centrium Healthcare Services).** After observing the autistic and cerebral palsy children at the physiotherapy department of the Hospital and how they lacked the ability to afford, l thought of starting an NGO. This was how **"Saarthi School for Special Children"** under the CSR sponsorship of Octaware started in 2010.

The manual physio and occupational therapy, their slow speed, inconsistency in the treatment, and required improvement led us to reach out to the Industrial Research and Consultancy Center at IIT Bombay to research the problem and provide the solution under the CSR of Octaware, which later converted into the company – **"Transpact MedTech."** I was delighted that with the twelve years of my journey with IIT Bombay, I was able to come up with a patented invention (**Vestibulator®**) when the entire world was lacking treatment and medical devices for autistic children. It is something which I am giving to my country and I believe the entire world will benefit from the product of India.

However, there were two challenges as well. On the primary, it was related to enhancement in the competencies as per the market need, and resistance to upgrading the competencies in the technical co-founding team was the obstacle. On a personal level, experiencing the challenge in running the business due to lack of financial knowledge was difficult at Octaware. Therefore, I focused on acquiring executive education with IIM Calcutta for a year, Harvard Business School, and Stanford Graduate Business School, which was again a one-year course. At Transpact, experiencing the challenge in product solutions due to lack of scientific research knowledge was an issue. Thus, I began the journey of research education with Lancaster University, and completed a PhD. Financially, We knew we had to provide a good salary to the employees. To address this challenge, we used the strategy of ESOP and started fundraising from the capital market.

At Octaware, we worked with a large set of clients in India and overseas. In India, the 1000 Bed COVID-19 Jumbo Centre in Mumbai adopted Octaware's hospital information management solution. The COVID-19 phase was a nightmare for the entire world, but I am happy that we could provide Oxygen concentrators, vaccines, blood test supplies, hospital beds and other necessities to everyone in need. In the USA, we developed the portal of the United Nations (UN) Foundation. In Saudi Arabia, we developed an enterprise solution for the Human Rights Commission. We deployed Forensic solutions at the Ministry of Interiors and Geographical Information system at the Ministry of Environment at Qatar. We implemented the Oil drilling solution for MB Petroleum in Oman. In Singapore, We deployed the ERP and Project management at Menarini Pharmaceutical. In Bangladesh, we worked with the Grameen Phone for a customer communication solution. We also organized multiple enterprise solutions deployed in other countries such as Australia, Philippines, Kuwait, Bahrain, Zimbabwe etc. At Transpact, we deployed the Vestibulator medical device at SRCC Children Hospital, Mumbai, Apang Kalyan Kendra in Pune benefiting thousands of children.

Choosing to follow my dreams helped me shape a better personality and obtain several awards too. At Octaware/IT firm, we are known best for our ethics and empathy as they are an integral part of our business, and our customers vouch for it. In Transpact/MedTech, our medical device is the first of its kind to address the vestibular stimulation needs of autistic and cerebral palsy. I have also been regarded for the innovative model of self-sustainability of the hospital while offering medical treatment to the spiritual leaders of the community irrespective of caste, creed, or religion. 10% of the cost is a unique model.

Some of my personal awards include being noted in the London World Book of Records in 2021 & Global Achievers Award for Talented Personalities, UAE in 2015. Octaware Technologies received the following awards—- Excellence in Compliance (SME) Award in 2020, Project of the Year – Contribution to the Community Award in 2020, CSR Project of the Year in 2017, Technology Provider of the Year in 2016, Contribution to Employment for Individuals with Disabilities in 2014, Best IT Product Architecture Award in 2013, Most Innovative Company of the Year in 2012, India's Top 50 Fastest Growing Company in 2011, Red Herring TOP 100 Asia Winner in 2010. On the other hand, Transpact received the Skoch Order-of-Merit award in 2019 and Young Innovator ZEE Award in 2018. The Centrium Healthcare Services was also awarded the prestigious International IFFSA Award in Maldives in the year 2019.

While being in the phase of my entrepreneurial journey and fulfilling my dream, I formed a few of my own thoughts to share with people who want to make a difference. I believe we can make a change, contribute to the lives of others, and bring positive change through purpose-driven entrepreneurship. I firmly preach that entrepreneurs are the changemakers in society determined to tackle the economic and social challenges of the nation. Moreover, business ideas are of little value in the business world. What matters is the execution with the right team having determination and devotion. Instead of building assets for yourself, one must try to become an asset of our society. I also believe that success is not what you gain or possess, but it is helping others become successful. Apart from the wisdom that I have gained, there are certain tangible achievements too that I acquired along the way.

I started the entrepreneurial journey with a capital of a mere USD 2,000/ and in just ten years, I managed to lead the company from inception to listing at the Bombay Stock Exchange (BSE) with a successful initial public offering. I became the holder of "London World Book of Records, UK" for the first time listing three organizations promoted by an individual at three different platforms of the Bombay Stock Exchange (BSE) of India in three consecutive years. I worked on the noble concept of creating employment for the blind and visually impaired people in the IT industry and successfully implemented the program for the first time in India. I also had the honour of leading a multi-sectoral business delegation accompanying the Hon. President of India and a member of a high-powered business delegation led by the Hon. Prime Minister of India.

This journey has changed my life in countless ways. I have become more patient and reflective on taking decisions. At this point in my life, I can never give up on discipline, reading, and learning. I am most passionate about social entrepreneurship and I enjoy working on the sustainability of social enterprises. Developing an innovative business model integrated with Corporate social responsibility to add value to society is something I constantly keep focusing on.

Apart from building my own business ventures, I also like volunteering in social activities. For example, the NGO RIDA Foundation, which I established with a group of young medical and corporate professionals, has been working in the slums of Mumbai since 2010. In May 2022, I joined my Alma Mater in Mumbai as a trustee of Anjuman-I-Islam established in 1874 with 97 institutions in Maharashtra and Executive Chairman of MH Saboo Siddik College of Engineering, Mumbai. I am always happy to serve and give back everything that I have imbibed throughout my life. I am also associated with two other non-profit organizations in Mumbai. On a personal level, I like to maintain a disciplined life too. I wake up ear;ly in the morning, walk 60 minutes after prayer, listen to one TED talk and start my work with a clear objective. When I am not working, I spend time with my NGO – RIDA Foundation where we work to provide accessible and affordable healthcare to slum dwellers of Mumbai and a rehabilitation center for cerebral palsy and autistic children.

I don't know if my words will help anyone, but if I could offer any advice to someone who is about to embark on a similar journey, then I would say that while doing business, one must make sure to use their brain (IQ) and heart (EQ) both. The mind helps you for vertical growth, and the heart is required for horizontal growth. Applying the mind may take one to a height, but in order to travel a long-distance application of the heart is required. You should never underestimate the person with whom you are interacting or negotiating in a business or personal relationship irrespective of what level he is. Always look for value, add the same for others and close for win-win situations. The almighty has always given something better than you in the other person.

Therefore, one must try to find that and learn from it or inculcate that quality and strength within yourself.

Everything that I am today is because of the sacrifices of my beloved father. For him, I have been privileged to attend executive education from five Ivy League Universities – Stanford, Harvard, Oxford, Cambridge, and MIT. As an executive Chairman of my Alma Mater, MH Saboo Siddik College of Engineering, I conceptualized and helped start an innovative ITI (Mechanic, A/C Technician) courses for Deaf and Mute students starting in July 2023. I am working on developing a technical skill and employability program for women with disabilities in the area of IT and Healthcare to generate a home-based employment and entrepreneurship ecosystem under my NGO – RIDA Foundation. I was invited as a speaker at Harvard Business School, USA in 2022, and IIT Bombay. I have started nine organizations since 2006, got listed 3 at BSE, ran 3 as Pvt Ltd, and failed in 3 ventures.

I believe failures are equally important in life. Unless you fail, you can never learn from your mistakes and rise again with a better hope towards the next phase. Even though I failed in the finance company which I co-founded, the private nursing institute for girls' paramedical education, and a nano-model medical center establishment; I learnt a lot from my downfalls. I have also been a member of the "Travelers' Century Club" and visited 140 countries and two hundred seventy world cities. Juggling through the disparities of life and still having faith and confidence to face any hurdle that occurs has helped me achieve my dream.

My father, a beacon of wisdom, has always guided me and my siblings to experience the world far and beyond. Like a seasoned mariner urging us to embark on an adventurous voyage, he compelled my siblings and me to face the unvarnished reality of the world and carve our own mark. His instruction was akin to sowing a potent seed of empathy in our hearts, which has since blossomed into a tree that provides shelter and comfort to those in need. I am happy with all the materialistic success, but at the same time I am overjoyed that I have been able to innovate something for the sake of my society. I have contributed not only to economic development but also in the social upliftment of my country. So, this was my story and how I did it. I dreamed of something in my childhood and it finally has come true. I hope you dream too and watch it turn true.

AUTHOR BIO

Dr. Mohammed Aslam Khan serves as the Chairman and Managing Director of Octaware Technologies Limited, an IT services and solution company present in 9 countries, embodying a blend of seasoned technologist and astute business acumen. Prior to establishing Octaware in 2005, Dr. Khan held key roles including Director at AskMe Corporation in Seattle, where he successfully launched its Indian subsidiary, later acquired by RealCom Software Inc, Japan. His career also includes pivotal contributions at Microsoft Corporation in the development of Windows2000 products and at Citibank N.A., Japan, focusing on financial trading software. Committed to social entrepreneurship, Dr. Khan has founded healthcare ventures and established the RIDA Foundation, dedicated to enhancing education and medical aid for the underprivileged. He champions innovation and entrepreneurship through initiatives like business incubators and accelerator facilities. All three of his ventures got listed on the Bombay Stock Exchange under different categories making the proud entry to the London World Book of Records, UK.

Academically accomplished, Dr. Khan holds degrees from prestigious institutions and has completed executive programs at renowned universities such as Stanford University, Harvard Business School, MIT, Oxford, and Cambridge University. Actively engaged in industry leadership, he serves on the Executive Committee of the Electronics and Computer Software Export Promotion Council sponsored by the Department of Commerce, Government of India, and has led significant business delegations worldwide.

DR. MOHAMMED ASLAM KHAN, CO-AUTHOR

7

CONQUERING THE UNKNOWN – THE INSPIRATIONAL TALE OF ENTREPRENEURIAL TRIUMPH

BY

PRASHANT PANIGRAHI

"Believe you can, and you're halfway there."

– Theodore Roosevelt

Picture this: a little boy plays without care beside his simple abode and resides in a place that hardly anyone else knows the name of. He spends his days striving to learn as much as he can from everything that life offers him, which is made difficult by the fact that he is on the move to new locales every few years.

Would you ever imagine such a boy growing up to become one of the most influential self-made thought-leaders of his time or leading multiple organizational units toward success over the span of only a couple of decades? Well, I did it all, and this is the story of how I did it all.

Let me show you my world, dear reader.

Get to Know Me

I was born to a humble family in Bhoipali, a quaint hamlet in Odisha. There must have been hardly 100 to 150 inhabitants in my ancestral village, and I grew up knowing most of them. That little hamlet I called home was the only world I knew for a long time, and little Prashant was utterly unaware that he was destined to be in much bigger places later in life.

Like nearly every teenager graduating during the Y2K boom for the Indian IT industry, I was swept away in the Information Technology wave right after my master's degree because the field was so wildly expanding in those years. Everyone I met was really into the new gizmos arriving on the market for public use. Telecommunication was improving by leaps and bounds, and the internet would creep into our lives in the next few years, too. Caught up in the frenzy, I decided to have a bite of the IT hotcake and build my career in that field.

Soon enough, with tons of hard work and some much-appreciated support from the Universe, I made my mark professionally and established my personal brand. I have always had a knack for devising innovative solutions to complex problems, which proved very useful during my career. I am adept at something called Systems Thinking, which involves making sense of the elaborateness of the world by looking at it as a whole and in terms of interconnected elements rather than dividing it into parts and individual pieces. Systems thinking has been used as a way of generating practical, result-oriented actions in complicated contexts, enabling a systems change, and I have been utilizing this concept in the processes I design for years together.

I also believe in and advocate for the holistic growth of an environment through its people, processes, and technology. Apart from these, I assist clients with enhancing business value through system alignment, integration, and change management. Through all my activities, I have passionately mentored many young leaders who have gone on to take the world by storm with their charisma and capabilities.

Professionally, I have been the most passionate about building a vibrant team of enthusiastic minds who come together with purpose-driven zeal and the grit to solve myriads of real-world issues and pursue various intellectual quests through technology. I thoroughly enjoy the dynamics of team building and systems thinking; I always aim to teach my proteges everything I know about these two crucial elements of problem analysis and resolution. This excites me immensely about my work and what I look forward to every new morning.

On the personal front, I am an ardent advocator of Smart Sage, a revolutionary concept that I conceptualized and religiously abide by. People say that if you are Smart, you cannot be Sage, and vice-versa. It implies that if you choose material success and charisma as your focus in life, you cannot simultaneously have compassion, equanimity, forgiveness, bliss, and inner tranquility. But I chose to prove this general assumption wrong. My lifelong mission has been to learn to exist simultaneously in Smartness and Sageness, i.e., embody invincible professional charisma and unchanging inner peace for a life of fulfillment that is also free of regrets. I have been successful in doing so for decades, and recognizing its importance, I decided to impart and advocate for the principles of Smart Sage to those who have the brightest brains and the greatest potential to master it.

Apart from this, I thoroughly enjoy the pursuit of becoming a better version of myself via various means, such as reading profoundly enlightening books and brandishing my flair for writing every day. I also devote a significant chunk of my time regularly to working on my shadow self, i.e., exploring the hidden blind spots of my personality, which, if handled well, could turn into my biggest strengths. On a warm Sunday afternoon, I enjoy indulging in lesser-taxing activities such as watching an entertaining TV show and spending quality time with my family.

My whole life has revolved around jumping from one uncharted territory to another, planting flags of my success wherever I've gone. From professional realms that were rarely explored to countries whose names I once hadn't even heard of, my fate took me everywhere I was meant to be. I've been there and done that. I've also been purposeful and successful, and I am proud of it.

So, you see, I am like you in many ways, dear reader — a regular person trying to do their bit for the world and live the most fulfilling life possible. I sincerely believe that all of us must remain learners at heart for the entirety of our lives, for only then will we be able to make the most of the little time we have been granted on this earth. I hope that knowing about my thoughts and reading about my life will help you with yours.

Where It All Began

My leadership journey began nearly a decade after I commenced my professional journey in the software industry. Thus, I will talk about my leadership in two phases, i.e., formative and individuation.

I like to call the first phase of my formative era "From the East to the West." In that phase, I embarked on the transition from comfort and complacency to exploration and growth by literally venturing into new territory. When I was in the first grade, trying to enjoy my childhood, I had to walk bare feet to my school, which was 2 km away. But by the time I shifted to Mumbai for my postgraduate degree, I had already traveled hundreds of miles away from the East to the West in what seemed to be the blink of an eye. Even my mode of conveyance changed over time: from arduous walks through dusty terrains as a child in Bhoipali to the bumpy rides on an old bicycle in the eastern part of India, then the tiresome journeys on crowded local trains in Mumbai (in the west of India), and all other phases in between. While my parents stayed in my birthplace, I would slog far away from them, trying to get a good education and make something of myself. There was even a time when, in my boyhood, there was no electricity till my 10th standard, so I literally burned the midnight oil and studied under the light of lamps.

After years and years of calling many places my home, it struck me one day that although, with each shift, I had gone further and further away from my hometown, I had never forgotten my roots or lost my identity. Also, with every shift, I established myself as the leader of my class and student union.

Before I moved to my individuation phase, I had successfully gained valuable experiences and exposure all the way from Bhoipali in India, the east (my birthplace), to Rockville in the USA, the west (my first overseas assignment), with thousands of miles in between.

The second phase I have christened is "From Mainframe to Metaverse." In this phase, I had to play the voyaging explorer again when starting my professional journey. My career bloomed in realms of technology that were relatively unknown at that time. I first ventured into Mainframe Technology in 1998 with TCS (Tata Consultancy Services). Then, I gradually moved on to even more novel-sounding fields, such as client-server, web, and ERP technologies.

Again, after finally entering my first leadership role in 2005, I was whisked away into yet another realm. I could no longer delve deeper into the technologies I was familiar with. Instead, I was exposed to the newest crop of technologies: IoT (Internet of Things), cloud computing, artificial intelligence, and the Metaverse. Once again, I dug my feet into the ground and mastered all those fields. Today, I am immensely proud to share that I have seen every technological trend rise and flourish as it came, and taken every advancement in my stride.

As you can see, dear reader, both these phases were united by one theme: adapting to change. A significant aspect of leadership as a realm is gracefully dealing with changes and fluctuations while turning every setback into a lesson. For me, it was difficult not to have a stable ground I could dig my feet into. As soon as I assumed there would be no further alterations in my life, I would be proven wrong. But the one thing that proved to be my saving grace was that I never laid my arms down. I took every twist and turn as it came, and that skill proved to be extremely useful throughout my leadership journey. I had a holistic life experience throughout my formative years, and it was quite a fun ride, flowing with the times and embracing challenges head-on. Everyone usually craves familiarity and stability, sticking to something they're good at and never really wanting to let go of that feeling. Not me, though. The only constant in my life has always been change, and I like it that way.

The Road I Ended Up Taking

One time, in the initial phase of my career, I was presented with two options for overseas assignments. I was grateful even to have been presented with a choice rather than being ordered to go without any say in the matter. That is why I was determined to make the best decision and set myself up for success. But there was a hiccup that made me feel like Robert Frost in his poem 'The Road Not Taken.'

The first option allowed me to lead a program from my home ground in the USA, where the onsite-offshore business model had been well established for the past few years. The second option was to lead a transformation and establish a brand new onsite-offshore model in an unexplored market, particularly Italy. Both these options were so attractive and exciting that I was caught in what seemed to be an inescapable dilemma. Although, if left to my own devices, I would immediately know what my heart would want me to do, I was confused by some of my seniors and colleagues who used this opportunity to pull my leg. They kept dangling a carrot in front of my eyes — of the wonderful life, rapid organizational growth, and overall benefits I would be able to savor if I stayed back and all the struggle and mental agony I would be subjected to if I chose to go to Italy. I'll be frank: I indeed was swayed by them for a bit.

The option that involved staying in the USA was definitely more convenient, with the added advantage of having a whole system ready for me to take over. However, to me, the option that would take me to Italy was the most exciting since I would get to set up a completely new system and would have to pioneer a delivery model in a fresh market with a high risk of failure. On one hand, many others were vying for the first option; on the other, there were no takers for the second. I'm sure they would have chosen convenience over a challenge if it was anyone else in my place. But you know me better by now, dear reader. My quest has always been to be different and make a difference no matter what. Of course, I chose the road less traveled to take a leap of faith and land in Italy.

The one thing that bolstered my inner voice and helped me take that momentous decision was the Smart Sage principle. Smartness is meaningless without Sageness, and I did not want to surrender to one without being balanced by the other. This brings me to a beautiful quote by psychiatrist and author Viktor. E. Frankl, "Between stimulus and response, there is a space. In that space, we have the power to choose our response. In our response lies our growth and our freedom." In my case, there was a space between two choices, and between those choices and my decision. I was surrounded by dilemmas and had multiple responses to the stimulus I was being provided. I could give in to the temptation and choose the easier way out. But I decided to answer my inner calling of choosing discomfort that would help me grow rather than the outer pressure of choosing comfort and social influence. I readily sacrificed the desire to enjoy the convenience of known territory in the USA for the quest to create new possibilities in an unfamiliar market in Italy. Embodying the concept of Smart Sage, I made my choice in the space between the stimulus and the response, and that is what helped me overcome my dilemmas.

The program I was leading in Italy was for establishing an IT outsourcing model in India for the 1st time. The challenges were multi-dimensional, i.e., the difference in language, resistance to change, shift from localization to globalization, etc. Also, as a young leader at 30, I had to lead an Italian team with an average age of 40. For me, it was a turbulent roller-coaster journey. But my Smart Sage spirit helped me navigate this journey with quest, zeal, and grit. This led to the successful establishment of the IO/IO model (Italy Onsite/India Offshore) or the IO-Square model, which was adopted in other TCS-Europe countries wherever there were language challenges.

There was another challenging leadership opportunity I was presented with soon after. I would potentially have to manage the

P&L (Profit and Loss) of a business unit globally, which means that I would have to deal with a lot of number crunching every day and even haul the business unit toward success. This role technically involved owning the e2e (end-to-end) value chain of the business, from creating the strategy blueprint to monitoring the results, just like an entrepreneur. There would be a ton of intimidating responsibilities on my shoulders, but internally, I felt ready to take on this role. That precise moment when I said yes to the opportunity is still a precious memory for me because, in that very moment, I decided to commit to the Smart Sage journey entirely (outer journey of Smart success and inner journey of blissful Sage) and never look back. This commitment helped me grow in multiple ways, personally and professionally, and to ceaselessly create value for my organization.

It fills me with pride to say that, in hindsight, I made the most sagely smart decision possible within the space between stimulus and response. That juncture in my career, where I chose to take the road not taken, became an inflection point for my transition into the leadership era of my career. To elaborate, the Smart aspect of decision refers to leveraging external insight and intelligence, whereas the Sagely aspect refers to leveraging spiritual intelligence of inner instinct. In simple terms, Smartness leverages the rational law of cause and effect, whereas Sageness leverages one's higher consciousness to cause the effect irrespective of the external/rational environment.

Training Wheels on My Cycle

Throughout your life, you must have seen children zooming around on their little bicycles with training wheels attached. Maybe you rode one yourself. Do you remember how those training wheels were used to help stabilize the bicycle, and you could ride much easier even if you didn't know how to balance it properly? Then, gradually, as you got better and better with balance, both training wheels would be removed one day, and you would be on your own after that. In my case, my mentors and guides were my training wheels, and life was my bicycle.

I am truly blessed to have had many people in my life who came by as guardian angels; they stood by my side and steered me through every challenge I encountered until I was ready to face more on my own. Among them, two people stand out as the greatest support in my professional life. I don't want to give too many details away for the sake of their privacy, but those two mentors meant everything to me back then, and they still do. They were the training wheels that taught me many things, and when the time came, quietly took the backseat while I defeated challenges on my own. I can never thank them enough.

During the initial phase of my leadership journey, while I was carving a place for myself, I was also undergoing a significant transformation on the personal front from bachelorhood to married life; the whole process could even be called change management. This involves mastering language, culture, personality, relationships, emotional intelligence, empathy, balancing stakeholder interests, and more. On one hand, I was trying to juggle multiple challenging tasks and projects as part of the program to produce Smart results. On the other hand, I was newly married, and my wife always expected the ideal aspects of me, i.e., making our life of unconditional love, by embracing the situations of inner weakness and outer challenges on our path; if any. She not only raised the bar for me but continuously supported and motivated me to be my ideal self for manifesting a successful, meaningful, and blissful partnership. Simply put, she endeavored to bring heaven into our endearing world. Thanks to her always raising the bar, I inculcated the habit of consistently trying to exceed my abilities and becoming a better version of myself at every opportunity, which also came in handy in my career to become Smart and Sage. Later, on the personal front, my wife became one of my biggest strengths and helped me wade through muddy waters unscathed. Also, I consider her my spiritual teacher who acts as a clear mirror to my shadow self, which helps me to become the best version of myself.

The change management wasn't easy to deal with. I faced much resistance, blame, and criticism from many people in the ecosystem. At one point in time, I felt that the very Universe was against me. That threw me off-balance and messed with the contentment I had. But my two mentors swooped in soon enough with their able guidance and valuable wisdom. To this date, I follow one of their pieces of advice to the T. They told me, "Be a Sage and do not give the remote control of your happiness to situations or people around you." Of course, I abided by their words and eventually graduated with flying colors from every instance of change management.

In other words, I faced flaws and fused failures in a Sagely Smart way. I will never forget my mentors and everything I learned from them. But, even before my wife and mentors came along in my life, my first and most influential mentors were the Buddha and Swami Vivekananda. True leaders in all their glory, I have considered them my most valuable idols or role models in my leadership journey.

The Buddha has taught us all that nothing in the world is permanent, and everything is transient. Everything around us will change, but we must also be careful not to get attached to that change. We have to embrace the impermanence and the flow of life. On the other hand, on entirely different lines, Swami Vivekananda asserted that spirituality without scientific development is meaningless. So, I eventually connected the dots, filled in the gaps, and adapted these teachings to my leadership/mentorship journey and the Smart Sage concept, respectively. The approach of facing flaws and fusing failures is aligned with the philosophical views of the Buddha and Swami Vivekananda. When I commenced my mentorship journey, I embodied all these learnings and presented them to my mentees for their upliftment.

I still ardently follow the teachings of these great spiritual leaders, and so do my other guiding lights — my wife and my mentors. All these figures together have created a lasting impact on the person I have grown to be. As I summarize it in a quote, "Mentors help you face your flaws and fuse your failures." This is exactly what all my mentors and well-wishers have done for me. They have unconditionally embraced me for who I am, my flaws and errors included, and helped me stand firm in times of adversity while motivating me to push ahead relentlessly.

A Success Story to Remember

At this point, you must be under the impression that the worst in my life was over, and I never really had many challenges to overcome after a certain point in time.

But let me remind you, dear reader, that change has been the only constant in everyone's life, so I would still come across many more hurdles and decisions to make. One of the toughest challenges I initially faced in my leadership journey was understanding and tackling the conformity culture enmeshed into the tapestry of an organization.

In a large organization, business excellence is driven by scores of policies, processes, procedures, and guidelines. These elements become guardrails to every task, transaction, activity, and behavior in the organizational ecosystem and are usually pretty watertight such that no loopholes can be found. Hence, every employee of the organization has to conform to these guardrails. This is known as conformity culture, where every employee is expected to think, talk, and do things the same way.

If someone wants to venture beyond the confines of policies, processes, procedures, and guidelines, they are immediately entangled in a net of justifications and explanations. That person would have to provide a full report on why they wish to change something in the ecosystem when it's working just fine. Also, before anyone even thinks about making a minor change to the existing guardrails, they have to keep the interests of the influential stakeholders in mind. This is because any nonconformity looks like a blot of ink in the audit report of those stakeholders till it is resolved with rationality and reason. In simple words, unconventional innovations or improvisations, which we Indians call 'jugaad,' are nearly impossible to get away with in a completely process-oriented culture. This very fact made it quite difficult for me to create the exponential business value that could be generated only by adopting unconventional and innovative measures for a process and thinking beyond standards and boundaries.

On one occasion, I received an opportunity that had the potential to help me grow my organization's business exponentially and create a great success story for the future. However, this particular opportunity was not in compliance with some of the internal guidelines of my business unit. Hence, initially, I was not allowed to pursue the competition that would award me the opportunity. Anyone else in my place would have been thrown off by this setback and not given it a second thought. However, this challenge intensified my grit and strengthened my quest to achieve what I had set out to achieve.

I was caught between the devil and the deep blue sea. Neither could I bypass the outer organizational guardrails (perceptual Sageness) monitored by influential stakeholders, nor could I resist the inner quest to tap the multi-million opportunity (Smartness).

I discussed my goal and action plan with the three top management layers to convince them to allow my participation in the competitive bid temporarily. First, I crossed the barrier of perceptual Sageness temporarily with a conditional commitment that I would establish compliance with internal guidelines within six months if I won the deal. Then, I vigorously burnt the midnight oil over the next few days, developed a business case to swoop them off their feet, and participated in the multi-million deal with a quest to create exponential business value. Fortunately for me, I was allowed to pursue the bid for the opportunity and do whatever had to be done. With full enthusiasm, my team and I took up the challenge and responded to the RFP with innovative solutions and value propositions. Finally, I won the deal against tough competition. But our task was still not over.

Then, I formed a vibrant team with the spirit of Smart Sage, i.e., a Smart effort to inspire customers' hearts. Again, we amped up our teamwork and worked relentlessly to exceed customer expectations, creating an inviting share for thought leadership in the customer ecosystem. We then convinced the targeted customers to adopt some of our preferred approaches (in alignment with internal guidelines) for business transformation, which they eagerly agreed to. Finally, we succeeded in complying with our internal guidelines and achieving high customer satisfaction. After just three months of the deal, we received 100% customer satisfaction in a survey, which gave us courage, zeal, and grit to pursue compliance with our organizational guidelines; better still, we made it all happen within six months of winning the deal as per our commitment. That moment was a celebration of the concept of Smart Sage for me and my vibrant team.

This transformation program I painstakingly executed eventually became a success story and a precedent for many other programs to follow, receiving many internal and external awards and accolades. It also turned out to be one of the most widely discussed programs. Eventually, the transformation program became an aspiring career destination for many organizational start performers. My heart was swollen with pride for a long time after that.

In corporate culture, performance evaluation is always a comparative exercise. So, when someone creates more value in an organization by following a nonstandard innovation (i.e., 'jugaad' in Hindi) amidst a conformity culture, it is always guaranteed to irritate many groups in the organization. So much so that the weaker section of the organization tries to protect the person's efforts as a matter of non-performance and non-aligned activity. Our collective success invited the ire of some of my peers, who were united by their envy of me.

Despite being directly subjected to the taunts of my peer groups, I continued to thrive and get better at my job. Through all the ups and downs, the one set of people I could count on for support, eyes closed, were my immediate supervisors who knew about my work from close quarters.

They had my back through every obstacle, meeting, and presentation, continuously pushing me to improve myself. Because of them, my belief in the transformative power of a healthy work environment was cemented, and I vowed to be one such change maker for the rest of my life.

Most IT-based organizations today function on a matrix or grid structure: domain-centric business units serve industry segments vertically, i.e., through different levels on the axis of increasing importance, whereas technology-centric business units serve horizontally across the industry segment, i.e., on the same level of a particular axis spanning multiple sectors within that segment. This differentiation is established to maintain the customer-centricity of the organization.

Generally, the domain units are more stable than the technology units. This is because computing technology has undergone significant overhauls and evolved nearly ten times in twenty-five years; I have pursued my career from the era of mainframe computing to the raging phenomenon called the Metaverse today. All of us know that during the emergence of a new set of technology, the old technology becomes merely a commodity and merges with vertical units. As the leader of every technology unit that came into existence one after the other, I have witnessed those technology units being dissolved and merged with vertical units every 2 or 3 years. Naturally, this meant that the nature of my job was always dynamic and never static, forcing me to keep up with the times and constantly upgrade my skills in order to walk toe to toe with every change that took place. I also had to build, restructure, and rebuild my team multiple times to create the best-performing squad equipped with the best-emerging technology. All this might not seem like much work, but I assure you that those involved always tried to pull the hair off our heads.

The initial few changes didn't bother me to the extent that the later ones did; I used to be so snowed under by my work that I started to feel like a victim of destiny. To be precise, I used to draw the analogy of bees who would work their limbs off to collect enough honey for the hive and then would suddenly lose all that honey every time the hive got damaged. Still, it does not feel hurt, disappointed, or discouraged, like a Sage, and builds another honeycomb in no time with Smartness, knowing that the second one, too, will remain temporarily and can be built again. Similarly, I almost gave up on my dream after a while, but then the Universe mysteriously carved out the Smart Sage path for me, and I was able to strike a balance between the warring factors to reach a reconciling and beneficial conclusion. Luckily, the bigger picture of Sagely Smartness rescued me from my misery, and I returned to my feet quickly every time.

I turned my problems into my strengths, eventually becoming stronger than the obstacles that came my way. Within no time, I had developed the expertise to quickly dismantle, assemble, and reassemble teams based on requirements and changing technologies. I had invested all my motivation into making system thinking, change, and adaptability a part of my DNA, allowing me to surf the most challenging waves in my professional life efficiently. I served all the verticals in my organization as internal customers, delivered successful transformation projects, and gave my Smartness and Sageness to everything assigned to me. This led to a holistic development of my Smart Sage personality, where I became an all-rounder not only in terms of the IT Industry but also in spiritual and practical aspects.

Parting Words

At one point, my professional achievements dazzled everyone like firecrackers do. I was getting promoted swiftly, winning awards one after the other, and achieving corporate targets tirelessly. Despite that, my colleagues had devised a nickname to tease me with: 'Pareshaan' Panigrahi. The word 'pareshaan' is a Hindi word indicating someone is distressed, restless, or bothered. Everyone except me could see that I was gradually losing my mind and becoming subservient to routines and schedules. All the success I had achieved in the material realm had not given me inner peace or fulfillment, which is why I later realized I was relying on Smartness and needed Sageness to come to my rescue. So, as soon as that realization struck me, I turned my life around bit by bit and reached a stage where Smartness and Sageness began to exist simultaneously in me. After that, I never faced any existential crises and began to make the most of my life enthusiastically. This is how great leaders are made: with patience, perseverance, and perspiration.

If there is one thing that has proven itself right at every phase in my life, it is that where there is a will, there is a way. Despite all the challenges that have arisen throughout my journey so far, I have been able to overcome them all solely because I never gave up on the spirit of Smart-Sage. This spirit did not stem from egoistic desire but from an inner quest. A quest is always driven by inspired activities with clarity in mind, purity in heart, and non-attachment to result. This is because once you are attached to the result, the clarity of mind and the purity of heart are lost within the negativity of fear, anger, hatred, doubt, and disbelief; these detrimental factors, in turn, become the impediments to manifesting results. This makes you neither Sage nor Smart.

Seeing hardships and major upheavals from close quarters, reflecting upon one's weaknesses, and putting in the maximum effort to turn those weaknesses into strengths makes a person as challenging and pure as a diamond. During my professional and leadership journey, one thing has been crystal clear: being successful without being purposeful is like having the most comfortable bed and yet tossing and turning from the lack of sleep at night. If you are not driven by a purpose or a goal that motivates you to strive for the greater good every day, then no matter how successful you become or how much fame and wealth you earn, you will never be able to lead a life of contentment and peace.

Meanwhile, if you wish to learn more about my life and my Smart-Sage lifestyle, read my book **'Smart Sage: Hacking your Shadow Self for High-resolution Lifestyle'** on Amazon. 'Smart Sage' is a transformative book that offers practical guidance on tapping into your inner wisdom and unlocking your full potential. It took me an entire decade of researching, practicing, experiencing, compiling, and condensing the learnings from my life, the philosophical teachings of the Buddha and other spiritual leaders, the concepts of system thinking I benefited from, and essential nuggets of wisdom into the principles of Smart Sage. In the book, I thus provide a framework for self-discovery and personal growth based on practices from experiential and experimental science, and it has received glowing reviews from accomplished and influential leaders worldwide.

With inspiring stories and insightful exercises, the book will help you better understand yourself and your purpose in life. Whether you want to overcome obstacles, achieve your goals, or live a more fulfilling life, 'Smart Sage' is the ultimate guide to unlocking your true potential and living your best life. I promise you that the hours you read the book will be one of the most meaningful and fruitful hours ever spent.

For the last bit of wisdom that I want to present to you, here are three pieces of advice that you must keep with yourself throughout your life: embrace the present moment with quest and grace, whether a challenge or opportunity; learn, unlearn, relearn; lastly, develop your consciousness as much as possible, for that makes human beings unique.

In the end, thanks to the blessings of all my well-wishers and my sincere efforts, I am where I am today, thriving on my leadership journey and spreading the light of knowledge wherever I go. I have been able to make a difference in hundreds of lives, singlehandedly navigate significant transformations, and become an invaluable part of the organization I have dedicated my entire life to. There is much left to do, and I will continue to do my best with the spirit of Smart Sage for the rest of my years.

Well, dear reader, this is "how I did it!" I hope, with a teeny bit of inspiration from my journey, you will too!

On the other hand, I was newly married, and my wife always expected the ideal aspects of me, i.e., making our life of unconditional love, by embracing the situations of inner weakness and outer challenges on our path; if any. She not only raised the bar for me but continuously supported and motivated me to be my ideal self for manifesting a successful, meaningful, and blissful partnership.

AUTHOR BIO

Mr. Prashant Panigrahi, after his master's in engineering, started his career in Tata Consultancy Services (TCS) during Y2K solution days. And currently, he is a global leader in digital and cloud technologies. As a consultant, he has served many fortune 500 organisations, including General Electric, Walgreen Boots Alliance, Nationwide, Woolworth, and Alphabet. He has demonstrated consistent excellence in business by leveraging his acumen in technology, self-leadership and six-sigma quality methodologies. In recognition of his transformational contributions, he has received several awards from CxO(s) of his employer and customers.

He has been an ardent researcher and partitioner of self-discovery and inner-wellbeing techniques for the last two decades; like Siddha Samadhi Yoga (SSY); based on teaching from Rishi Prabhakar; who was a disciple of Maharishi Mahesh Yogi (founder of Transcendental meditation movement) and guru of Sadhguru Jaggi Vasudev. He is also a practitioner of Vipassana meditation based on teachings of Buddha and a certified counsellor of the Dianetics technique, which intends to clear historical unconscious negative energy blocks called engrams.

His lifestyle promotes creating transformational business outcomes without compromising inner-wellbeing and meaning in life, which is an aspiring and inspiring dimension for many professionals in the rat race of the 21st century. Additionally, he is a system thinker and loves to connect the standalone dots to discover the meaning of life in every situation. He brilliantly blends the East's ancient experiential wisdom with the West's contemporary success principles. Hence, colleagues in his proximity call him an executive-yogi or corporate monk. In his personal life, he is a purpose alchemist and self-actualization coach. He spends his leisure time as an "ally in service" to people(s) with quest for a lifestyle of success along with purpose.

PRASHANT PANIGRAHI, CO-AUTHOR

ABOUT THE AUTHOR

This is a book written by industry experts, each contributing a chapter. Here's a list of all the CO-AUTHORS of this publication (in no particular order):

Dr. Santosh Batni
Narendra Ram
Anu Wakhlu
Shravan Gupta
Deepak Mohla
Dr. Mohammed Aslam Khan
Prashant Panigrahi

Published by: Raam Anand

* 9 7 8 1 9 5 7 4 5 6 5 2 2 *